About the Author

Dr Sandy Primrose MBE PhD has spent his professional life as a biologist in academia and industry, as well as working with various government agencies on food fraud and related topics. He is a keen gardener and passionate teacher and lectures extensively on plant-related topics.

Plants, Murder
and Medical Mysteries

To Janet & Donald

With best wishes

Sandy

Sandy Primrose

Plants, Murder
and Medical Mysteries

Olympia Publishers
London

www.olympiapublishers.com
OLYMPIA PAPERBACK EDITION

A CIP catalogue record for this title is
available from the British Library.

ISBN: 978-1-78830-886-1

First Published in 2021

Olympia Publishers
Tallis House
2 Tallis Street
London
EC4Y 0AB

Printed in Great Britain

Dedication

This book is dedicated to my wife who has had to listen to the stories herein, on far too many occasions.

Contents

PLANT NAMES AND PLANT FAMILIES

No knowledge of botany is required in order to enjoy this book and the use of botanical terms has been kept to an absolute minimum. However, the plants themselves are always identified by their scientific name which takes the form of a Latin binomial, e.g. *Hyacinthoides non-scripta*. The first part of the name, '*Hyacinthoides*' denotes the genus, i.e. it is the generic name. The second part, '*non-scripta*' denotes the species. This is the plant that many British people will know by its common name which is the English bluebell. So, you might ask, why not just use the common name? The reason is quite simple. Scientific names are constant across the world whereas common names are not. For example, as noted above, in England the bluebell is *Hyacinthoides non-scripta* but it can be confused with the Spanish bluebell (*Hyacinthoides hispanica*) which looks very similar to the inexpert eye. In Scotland, the bluebell is an entirely unrelated plant, *Campanula rotundifolia*, which in England is called a harebell. To add to the confusion, in Australia bluebells are the plant known as *Wahlenbergia communis* and in the United States they are species of *Mertensia*. So if someone talks about bluebells, it is not clear to which plant they are referring. Use the Latin scientific name and there is no doubt whatsoever.

Plants that share many features are grouped into families whose names always end with 'aceae', e.g. Asteraceae,

Fabaceae, etc. In the case of flowering plants, it is the structure of the flower that determines the family. For example, the Asteraceae is often referred to as the daisy family because all the plants in the family have flower structures that are very similar to that of the common daisy (*Bellis perennis*). The Fabaceae is often known as the pea family because all members have the same characteristic flower structure. In some cases, the flower structure might not be immediately apparent. For example, clovers (*Trifolium* species) belong to the Fabaceae but do not appear to have a pea-shaped flower. Look more closely and you will see that what people call the flower in a clover, is really a mass of tiny but characteristic pea-shaped flowers.

PART ONE:
THE START OF FORENSIC BOTANY

THE PIONEERING CASE: FINDING WHO KILLED BABY LINDBERGH

Charles Lindbergh was an American aviator who in 1927 went from obscurity as a US Air Mail pilot, to instantaneous world fame whilst only twenty-five years of age. What did he do? He won the Orteig prize by making the first non-stop flight from New York to Paris, a prize that had eluded many other more experienced pilots on both sides of the Atlantic. He flew a single-engine plane, called the Spirit of St. Louis, with no navigational aids and when he landed at Le Bourget airfield nearly thirty-four hours later, he was greeted by a crowd of 150,000 people. Such was his achievement at the time that he was awarded the US Medal of Honor (via a special Act of Congress), the Distinguished Flying Cross, the Congressional Gold Medal and the French Légion d'honneur. Time magazine made him their first Man of the Year and to this day he remains the youngest person to receive that accolade. As one person wrote at the time, "People are behaving as though Lindbergh had walked on water, not flown over it". However, all this fame was to have a price, and a deadly one at that.

In 1929, Charles Lindbergh married Anne Morrow and they went on to have six children. The first child was born in 1930 and was named after his father: Charles Augustus Lindbergh Jr. On March 1 1932, Charles Jr. was just twenty months of age when he was kidnapped from his parents' house in Hopewell, New Jersey. The child's absence was noted at about ten p.m. by his nurse. A search of the premises was made and a ransom note demanding $50,000 was found on the window sill of the nursery. A detailed search of the house and grounds found nothing of any interest or value except a wooden ladder under the nursery window. This ladder was in two sections and one of the two sections was split where it joined the other, suggesting it had broken during the ascent or descent.

Whilst the police continued their investigation, the kidnapper sent new ransom notes every few days. Eventually, using a newspaper as a means of communication, a go-between was agreed by Lindbergh Sr. and the kidnapper: he was Dr John Condon, a retired New York school principal. Following the delivery of the sixth ransom note, Condon met an unidentified man calling himself 'John'. Following this meeting Condon received a seventh ransom note and a baby's sleeping suit as a token of identity. The Lindberghs confirmed that the sleeping suit was the one that had been worn by Charles Jr. More ransom notes were received and on April 2 the twelfth note was delivered to Condon. Following the instructions in it he met 'John' and paid him $50,000 in return for information stating that the baby was on a boat called 'Nellie' in Martha's Vineyard, Massachusetts. No boat with that name was found following an intensive search.

On May 12 1932, the body of the kidnapped baby was found by accident. The body was partially buried and badly decomposed. The head had been crushed, there was a hole in the skull and some body parts were missing. Forensic examination suggested that the child had been dead for about two months and that death was caused by a blow to the head.

Up until the discovery of the body, the FBI had been acting in an auxiliary role as they had no federal jurisdiction. On May 13 there was major change: the US President directed that the FBI should take control of the investigation.

The first thing that the FBI did was to ask all the banks in the greater New York area to keep a close watch for the ransom money. This was a very clever move because $40,000 of the ransom money had been paid in gold certificates. These certificates were a form of paper currency in denominations of $10 and $20 that gave the holder title to a corresponding amount of gold coin but could only be redeemed for gold via a bank. The second thing that the FBI did was to get the ransom notes examined by handwriting experts. These experts were of the unanimous opinion that all the notes were written by the same person and that the writer was of German nationality but had spent some time in America. Finally, a wood expert was called in to examine the ladder found at the crime scene. That expert was Arthur Koehler from the Forest Service Division of the United States Department of Agriculture.

On May 2 1933, The Federal Reserve Bank of New York discovered 296 ten-dollar gold certificates and one $20 gold certificate which had been part of the ransom money. These had been made as a single deposit by "J.J. Faulkner, 537 West 149th Street". Despite extensive investigation this depositor was not found. In early 1934, President Roosevelt issued a proclamation that required all gold and gold certificates to be returned to the Treasury. For a period of seven months after the proclamation none of the outstanding gold certificates from the ransom were recovered. Then, starting on August 20 and extending into September, a total of 16 gold certificates from the ransom turned up in various New York locations. The depositor was not known.

The breakthrough came on September 18 1934. A bank contacted the FBI to say that one of the ransom gold certificates had just been deposited. It soon was ascertained that this certificate had been received from a gasoline station. It had been given in return for five gallons of gasoline. However, the pump attendant had been suspicious and had noted down the license plate of the automobile whose tank had been filled. This automobile was registered to Bruno Hauptmann of 1279 East 22nd Street in the Bronx, New York. Hauptmann's house was put under surveillance and when he emerged and got into the suspect automobile he immediately was arrested.

When questioned whilst in custody Hauptmann admitted to being a carpenter from Saxony in Germany and having been in America for approximately eleven years — an exact match for the profile generated by the handwriting experts who had examined the ransom notes. Hauptmann's handwriting was compared with that on the ransom notes and found to be remarkably similar. Next, Dr Condon who had acted as the intermediary between the Lindbergh family and the kidnapper identified Hauptmann as the 'John' that he had met. Finally, when the police searched Hauptmann's residence they found ransom certificates with a value of $13,000. They also found Dr Condon's telephone number scrawled on a door frame inside a cupboard. Further investigation revealed that he had not worked as a carpenter since March 1 1932, which was the date of the kidnapping. There now was enough evidence to charge Hauptmann with larceny but there was no concrete evidence that Hauptmann had been involved in the kidnapping of baby Lindbergh. That would be provided by the wood expert, Arthur Koehler.

Koehler had begun investigating the wooden ladder found at the scene of the crime long before Hauptmann was arrested. The ladder had been crudely built but showed signs of having been built by someone used to working with wood. It was in three parts and could be disassembled to fit in a car. Using microscopic analysis of the wood grain it was found that four different types of wood had been used: yellow pine, Ponderosa pine, Douglas fir and birch. The wood comprising the top left rung of the ladder clearly had been used before. It had been sawn from a bigger piece and there were nail holes that had been made by old-fashioned square nails. Koehler advised the authorities to look for a missing board in any place connected with a suspect.

By examining the ladder with oblique light in a darkened room, Koehler was able to see marks that suggested some of the timber had been smoothed with a commercial planing machine and some with a hand planer. He requested planed wood samples from more than 1,500 lumber mills across the country. A sample from Dorn Lumber in McCormick, South Carolina had plane marks identical to some of those on the ladder. From there, Koehler traced the wood used in the ladder to the National Lumber and Mill Work Company in the Bronx, that happened to be just ten blocks from Hauptmann's house.

During the search of Hauptmann's house, a hand planer was found. Koehler was able to show that this produced markings on wood identical to some of those found on the ladder. Then, a week after the arrest, police realised that one of the floor boards in Hauptmann's attic had been partly cut away. Koehler was able to show that the wood used in the top left rung had been cut from the attic board; there was a perfect match of the annual rings in the wood and the nail holes matched those in the floor joists. These findings directly linked Hauptmann to the kidnapping.

The trial of Hauptmann began on January 3 1935 and lasted five weeks. On February 13, almost three years from the date of the kidnapping, the jury returned a verdict: guilty of first-degree murder. The sentence was death. Hauptmann's lawyer lodged an appeal but in December 1935 the Supreme Court of the State of New Jersey upheld the conviction. A petition for clemency was dismissed and on April 3 1936 Hauptmann was executed in the electric chair. Following the execution there were claims that Hauptmann had been convicted unfairly: the defence lawyer was an inadequate drunkard, the police and FBI had fabricated evidence, the identification of Hauptmann by Dr Condon had not been done using an identity parade, etc. These claims continued to be made sporadically up until the present time. What is most satisfying is that nobody has ever challenged the analysis of the wood undertaken by Arthur Koehler, even though it was the first time that this kind of forensic analysis had been undertaken. Regardless of the veracity of the evidence presented to show that Hauptmann was involved in the kidnapping of baby Lindbergh, there was no evidence that showed that he killed the child. However, as there was no evidence that Hauptmann had an accomplice it was assumed that he had committed the murder as well.

Why was the abduction of baby Lindbergh a 'pioneering case' as the chapter title infers? Prior to the Hauptmann trial there was little use of scientific expert witnesses and certainly not botanists. The defence lawyer argued strongly against allowing Arthur Koehler to testify. He said, "There is no such animal known among men as an expert on wood; that it is not a science that has been recognised by the courts; that it is not in a class with handwriting experts, with fingerprint experts, or with ballistic experts... The witness probably may testify as an experienced carpenter or something like that... but when it comes to expressing an opinion as an expert or as a scientist, why that is quite different indeed. We say that the opinion of the jurors is just as good..." In an historic moment for forensic botany the judge replied, "I deem this witness to be qualified as an expert". It would be another sixty years before forensic botany was used again as evidence in a criminal trial. It now is being used more and more (see Section 4) but has a long way to go before it can match the use of DNA profiling.

Australia's version of the Lindbergh killing

The Sydney Opera House is one of the 20th century's most famous and distinctive buildings and now is a UNESCO World Heritage Site. Most of the eight million people who visit the site annually know little of its troubled history that included major construction delays and the resignation of the architect. Initially an appeal fund was set up to raise the A$7 million that the building was estimated to cost. When this appeal only raised A$900,000 the Premier of New South Wales introduced the Opera House Lotteries. Tickets cost $10 and the first prize was A$100,000 (equivalent to A$3 million today). The first lottery was drawn in January 1958 and it was July 1975 before the lottery had raised the A$102 million that it ultimately cost to complete construction of the Opera House.

Lottery number ten was drawn on June 1 1960 and the first prize of A$100,000 was won by Bondi resident Bazil

Thorne. In 1960, there was no conception of the need for privacy of lottery winners and details of the lucky Thorne were published in the Sydney newspapers. The reports also revealed that the prize would be paid on Thursday 7 July. On the morning of 7 July, Bazil's son Graeme Thorne left home at 8.30 a.m. to walk three hundred metres to the home of a family friend, who would drive him to school along with her sons. Graeme Thorne never arrived at the friend's house and it was soon ascertained that he had disappeared.

Graeme's disappearance was reported to the Bondi police and a sergeant went to the boy's home to investigate. Whilst there, about 9.40 a.m., the sergeant took a threatening telephone message from a male with a foreign accent. The caller was demanding $25,000 before 5 p.m. that day for the boy's safe return or else, "… the boy will be fed to the sharks". The caller made no plans for the delivery of the money but said that he would make further contact. He rang again at 9.47 p.m. and, after enquiring if the money was available, gave instructions for it to be placed in two paper bags. The caller then hung up and made no further demands. Unfortunately, different police officers answered the two calls from the kidnapper, and both claimed to be the boy's father. A newspaper account of the return of the boy's father from another city would have confirmed to the kidnapper that the police were involved.

Investigators soon had two pieces of evidence that were to prove important in the conviction of the kidnapper when ultimately he came to trial. First, some weeks before the kidnapping a foreign man had called at the Thorne residence making enquiries about their new telephone. Multiple witnesses reported seeing the same man at numerous times in the park opposite the Thorne's house. Second, about 8.20 a.m. on the day of the kidnapping, some witnesses had seen an iridescent blue 1955 Ford Customline double-parked on the route that Graeme Thorne would have followed. Although 5,000 vehicles matching this description were registered, the police interviewed all of the owners.

A few days after Graeme disappeared, his school case and his school cap were found but there was no sign of his body. Then, six weeks after the kidnapping, his body was found where it had been hidden on vacant land in the suburb of Seaforth. The body was wrapped in a woollen rug. Graeme was dressed in the clothes that he had been wearing when he left for school. His ankles were tied together with a piece of twine. There was a scarf tied around his neck and the size of the scarf loop indicated that it had been used as a gag. An autopsy revealed that death was caused either by major head trauma or asphyxia and many other factors suggested that death occurred within twenty-four hours of the kidnapping.

Closer examination of the rug in which the body had been wrapped yielded a number of vital pieces of evidence. First, a number of animal hairs were found and certain features of these suggested that they had come from a Pekingese dog. Second, human hairs were found that had come from a woman with blonde hair or grey hair that had been colour rinsed. Some plant foliage also was found and this was shown to come from two shrubs: *Chamaecyparis pisifera var. Squarrosa* and *Cupressus glabra*. Neither of these conifers was growing on the allotment where the body was found but one of them was growing in a nearby garden. Examination of the clothing from the body revealed the presence of pink limestock mortar. The distribution of this indicated that Graeme had been lying on his back near or under a brick building when the scarf was tied around his neck. Because of the pink colour of the mortar and the presence of the two garden conifers, neither of which are indigenous to Australia, it was inferred that the building was a domestic residence.

Police began searching for a house with a blue Ford Customline car, pink mortar and with the two different conifers growing in the garden. Following a tip-off from a postman, police visited a house in Moore Street in the suburb of Clontarf, about three kilometres from where Graeme's body had been found. The house was constructed of bricks bound with pink mortar, built on a high foundation and with a garage under the front of the house. Access to the foundation could be gained from an opening in the rear wall of the garage. A search beneath the house showed that the soil was impregnated with fragments of pink mortar. Crucially, on either side of the garage door were specimens of *Chamaecyparis pisifera* and *Cupressus glabra*.

The house had been occupied by a Hungarian immigrant named Stephen Bradley. He spoke with a foreign accent, had a Pekingese as a family pet and his wife had dyed blonde hair. However, the house had been sold and arrangements had been made for the furniture to be removed at 11 a.m. on the day that Graeme was abducted. Bradley's wife and children had been seen leaving the house at 10 a.m. on the same day. The Bradleys had moved to the suburb of Manly, but by the time the police had this information the Bradley family had already left Australia for London aboard SS Himalaya. Examination of many household items and the car revealed the presence of hairs identical to those found with Graeme's body. Police also recovered a tassel that matched one that was missing from the rug in which the body had been wrapped. So, the police set off in pursuit of Bradley and when the SS Himalaya docked in Colombo he was taken off the ship and extradited to Sydney.

When Bradley arrived back in Sydney he was put in an identification parade. Mrs Thorne picked out Bradley as the man who had called at her door making enquiries about her new telephone. Other witnesses identified Bradley as the man that they had seen sitting in the park opposite the Thorne home. Bradley went on trial in March 1961, was found guilty and sentenced to life imprisonment. The criminal fraternity has a loathing of individuals who violate children and so Bradley had to be isolated from the other prisoners until his death from a heart attack in 1968.

PART TWO:
A MISCELLANY OF MEDICAL MYSTERIES

THE AGONY AND THE ECSTASY

In the late '60s I was a graduate student at university in northern California. It was a great time to be living there, it was the hippie era and everyone was having fun. It also was the time when the recreational use of drugs became commonplace. Walking around parts of San Francisco, or even the Berkeley campus of the University of California, one could nearly get high from the fumes of marijuana. Someone, supposedly Charlie Fleischer, said that if you could remember the 60s you really weren't there. As I can remember them, was I there? About this time, reports appeared in the underground press that it was possible to get high by eating seeds of the flowering plant known as morning glory (*Ipomoea tricolor*). Everyone said, "How strange," and we thought no more about it. Little did I realise that there was a close link to a mysterious disease that had begun ravaging Europe over 1,000 years earlier.

Saint Anthony's Fire

A great plague of swollen blisters consumed the people by a loathsome rot, so that their limbs were loosened and fell off before death. Annales Xantenses 857 AD

In France, starting about the 6th century, there were repeated plagues of a disease that is aptly described in the above quotation. Between 591 and 1789 there were over one hundred and thirty episodes. In affected people, the condition would start with a pricking sensation in their arms or legs. This would turn to burning pain, the limb would swell and redden and then turn gangrenous, before dropping off. The afflicted were lucky (!) if the limb died without taking its owner with it. After killing and maiming thousands of people, the disease would disappear for no apparent reason and might not return for tens of years. The largest known outbreak was in 944 and killed over forty thousand people across France.

Most of the affected would have been simple peasants and so they turned to the Church for help. Many would pray to Saint Anthony, a third century ascetic from Egypt who suffered from visions in which he battled against the devil. They would visit abbeys and other sacred sites associated with the saint in the hope of curing themselves. This led to the disease being known as Saint Anthony's Fire. The other name for the disease was Holy Fire because of the belief that it was a punishment from God. During an outbreak near Grenoble in 1095, a wealthy Frenchman called Gaston de la Valloire founded a hospital dedicated to the care of victims of St. Anthony's Fire. This hospital was staffed by monks and this led to the establishment of the Order of Hospitallers of St Anthony. The monks belonging to the order wore black robes with a blue logo or badge, in the form of the Greek letter tau. Each hospital was painted red to inform the illiterate that aid was available to alleviate their suffering.

The order established monasteries that acted as hospitals across France. Some of these hospitals, like the one at Lavardin in the little Loir valley, were decorated with frescoes depicting St. Anthony and sufferers from St. Anthony's Fire.

Others had richly decorated altarpieces that depicted Christ suffering on the cross. The idea, supposedly, was that patients would look at Christ's suffering and think that their condition was not so bad after all! One of the most famous altarpieces is the 16th century one by Matthias Grunewald, that was commissioned by monks in the monastery at Isenheim around 1508. As well as depicting the crucifixion, it features a tortured St. Anthony. Around 1501, the Dutch artist Hieronymus Bosch painted the Triptych of the Temptation of St. Anthony. Among the many grotesque images in the triptych are an amputated foot and a half-vegetable half-human figure, representing madness, another side of St Anthony's Fire. This figure is painted in the shape of a mandrake root which is interesting for this root (see p77) was used by the monks to alleviate the pain of St. Anthony's Fire. Perhaps most gruesome of all, until the beginning of the 18th century the mummified limbs of victims were housed in the Church of Saint Anthony at La-Motte-Saint-Didier.

The Order of St. Anthony expanded from France into Germany and Scandinavia and gained wealth and power as grateful patrons bestowed money and charitable goods to the hospitals. By the end of the Middle Ages there were three hundred and ninety-six settlements and three hundred and seventy-two hospitals owned by the Order. Initially, the monks could remove gangrenous limbs and treat open sores but later these tasks were given to barber surgeons. Various remedies were used to treat the disease symptoms and salves were invented to treat the associated skin disorders. Once the cause of the disease was identified (see below) in the 17th century, the Order of St. Anthony began to decline and in 1776 it was incorporated into the Order of the Knight Hospitaller

(Maltese). Details of the recipes used to treat St. Anthony's Fire were lost and so it is not possible to know how effective they would have been.

A German physician by the name of Thelius documented an outbreak, that occurred in Hesse in 1596. He attributed the cause to consumption of diseased grain, but little notice was taken. It was 1670 before the cause of St. Anthony's Fire was identified and the credit for this goes to a French physician called Thuillier. He made some key observations. First, it was a disease of the countryside and not urban areas even though the latter were crowded and unsanitary. Second, it did not appear to be contagious. Third, patients in the hospitals usually recovered albeit without some limbs. Finally, and most important of all, the wealthy generally were not affected, money could buy one's freedom from the disease. Eventually he reached the conclusion that St. Anthony's Fire must be linked to diet. His next challenge was to identify the causative dietary constituent.

He noted that rye bread was a staple foodstuff in poor households but that city dwellers ate the more expensive white bread that was made from wheat. Furthermore, hospitals did not serve rye bread and the health of the patients improved in hospital. But what was it about rye bread that caused the problem? The answer came to him one day while he was walking in the country. Passing a field of rye, he noted what the farmers called cockspurs on the cereal heads. Cockspurs get their name because of the resemblance between them and the spurs on the legs of roosters. As a doctor he knew of the use of these cockspurs to hasten childbirth. Their use for this indication even appeared in the 1836 Dispensatory of the United States. These cockspurs were so common on rye that they were thought to be a normal part of the plant. When rye flour was made it included ground cockspurs. Farmers did not believe Thuillier, or perhaps they did not want to listen to him: rye is a cereal that can survive cold and wet conditions much better than wheat and can grow on marginal land. Nevertheless, Thuillier's discovery signalled the beginning of the decline in incidents of St. Anthony's Fire.

Edmond Tulasne was a French lawyer who developed an interest in plants and fungi. In 1853 he was studying the cockspurs from rye and discovered that they were part of the reproductive cycle of a fungus that infects the rye flowers. The fungus is called ergot which is derived from the Old French word 'argot' meaning 'cockspur'. The scientific name for the ergot fungus is *Claviceps purpurea*. The cockspurs are known as sclerotia and they help the fungus to over-winter. Rye is the most winter hardy of all cereals and is normally sown in late summer or early fall. Infection of rye with the ergot fungus is favoured when extremely cold winters are followed by very wet summers. As these climatic conditions only occur sporadically, it is possible to explain why there could be many years between outbreaks of St. Anthony's Fire.

Since the Middle Ages rye has been cultivated widely in central and eastern Europe, especially along what today is the French-German border, Poland, Hungary and European parts of Russia. In the rest of Europe, it was cultivated only on marginal land. This explains why the outbreaks of St. Anthony's Fire, were largely restricted to France and Germany. Britain escaped the disease because rye was only cultivated in a few, localised parts of England. Robert Burns wrote a poem entitled 'Comin' Thro' the Rye', which many people think implies that rye was grown in Scotland. It was not. The 'Rye' to which Burns refers was a small stream in his home county of Ayrshire.

Work done in the early 20th century by chemists revealed that the ergot fungus produces a large range of compounds which are known as ergot alkaloids. Some of these alkaloids cause vasoconstriction and excessive ingestion of them will result in a diminished flow of blood to the extremities. The outcome will be gangrene, which was the condition affecting the unfortunate souls who had St. Anthony's Fire. Other ergot alkaloids have psychoactive effects and the best known of these is lysergic acid (LSD). This was made famous by Harvard psychologist Timothy Leary ("Turn on, tune in, drop out.") and by the Beatles ('Lucy in the sky with diamonds'). LSD-types of alkaloids might have caused some of the symptoms of those suffering from St. Anthony's Fire.

The witches curse

The trouble began in Salem, Massachusetts in January 1692. Eight young girls became ill. The first were 9-year-old Elizabeth Parris, the daughter of the Reverend Samuel Parris, and her cousin Abigail Williams who was 11-years-old. Their sickness was unlike any other known to the residents. The girls suffered from delirium, violent convulsions, incomprehensible speech, trance-like states and odd skin sensations. Soon it was decided that witchcraft was involved, and this led to prejudices being exposed.

The first to be accused was Tituba, the Parris's Caribbean-born slave. Next were two elderly women, Sarah Good and Sarah Osburn, who were considered to be of ill repute, they were stereotypical of witches in that period. Later, even covenanting members of the church were accused. Ultimately, over one hundred and fifty people were arrested as witches. By September 1692, twenty men and women had been put to death and five others had died in jail. None of the executed confessed to witchcraft even though doing so would have saved their lives. On October 29, the governor of Massachusetts ordered the witch trials to end, leaving the people of Salem to question who had been afflicted by madness: the victims or the accusers.

In 1976 an American psychologist, Linda Caporael, published an article in the respected journal Science. In this article, she suggested that the girls in Salem might have been suffering from convulsive ergotism. The symptoms displayed by the afflicted girls certainly fitted with the known effects of the psychoactive ergot alkaloids. Caporael also noted that children and pregnant women are most likely to be affected by ergotism and that individual susceptibility varies greatly.

Rye was the most reliable of the Old World grains and was well-established in New England at the time of the witchcraft incident. Because of the bitter winters, spring sowing was the rule and summer rye is more prone to sclerotia formation than winter rye. Harvesting would take place in August and the grain was stored in barns until it was threshed around Thanksgiving. The pattern of weather in 1691 was perfect for an ergot infestation: early rains and warm weather in the spring progressed to a hot and stormy summer. Any ergot infected rye flour would start to be made into bread in late 1691 and early 1692 — just when the problem arose in Salem.

Many people have challenged Caporael's suggestion that ergotism was at the root of the witchcraft trials. However, they have failed to provide an alternative explanation. As Caporael herself said, "… there can never be hard proof for the existence of ergot in Salem, but a circumstantial case is demonstrable". There is one piece of evidence that favours ergotism, that is not mentioned by Caporael. The records of the witch trials state that some of the accused had been eating red bread. It is known that when the sclerotia of the ergot fungus are milled they produce a dark red flour. If present in rye flour at a level of 10% or more this will result in red bread!

The tragedy at Pont-Saint-Esprit

By the early 20th century enough was known about the dangers of ergot-infected rye that procedures for its control had been developed. Fields that have contained infected crops are deeply ploughed to bury any sclerotia. This stops their germination and they will die within twelve months. A different crop, one that is not susceptible to ergot, is sown the following year. This will break the cycle of any ergot that may have survived the previous year's ploughing. Even when infected rye has been harvested, it is possible to separate the sclerotia from the rye seeds using a flotation method. Despite this knowledge there still have been outbreaks of ergotism in developed countries. One in Russia in 1926–7 resulted in ten thousand cases and there were two hundred cases among central European Jewish immigrants in England in 1927. However, the worst modern outbreak occurred in the little French town of Pont-Saint-Esprit in Provence.

Jean Vieu was a doctor in Pont-Saint-Esprit. On August 12 1951, he saw two patients who were complaining of intense pain in their lower abdomen. At first he thought that they had acute appendicitis but he was puzzled by some of the other symptoms displayed by the patients: low body temperature and cold fingertips. Then the patients started hallucinating. The next day he saw another patient with the same symptoms. He was concerned enough to consult two other local doctors, only to discover that between them they had twenty patients with the symptoms described above.

By August 14 the number of patients had increased and the town's hospital was filled to overflowing. The patients had to be tied to their beds to stop them running mad through the streets. One man tried to drown himself whilst screaming that his belly was being eaten by snakes. Another jumped out of a second-floor window shouting that he was an aeroplane. One boy tried to strangle his grandmother. All available strait jackets were rushed to the town to restrain the victims of whatever sickness was affecting them. By the time the disease petered out, over three hundred had been affected and there were thirty-two cases of insanity plus five deaths.

Public health officials had been trying to discover the cause of the dementia that they were sure was some kind of food poisoning. The symptoms were not consistent with any known infection so probably were chemical in origin. The only foodstuff that all of the victims had eaten was bread from a particular baker. So, samples of this bread were sent for analysis and it was found to contain over twenty ergot alkaloids. This result was consistent with the symptoms displayed by the victims: they had convulsive ergotism. However, there still was a puzzle. The bread had been made with wheat flour so there should not have been any ergot alkaloids in it. It transpired that a farmer had a batch of contaminated rye and he sold it to a miller who mixed it with wheat and ground it into flour. This flour then was sold to a baker in Pont-Saint-Esprit who turned it into the bread that set off the outbreak of madness. However, that is not the end of the story.

Hank Albarelli is an American investigative journalist who wrote a book called 'A terrible mistake: the murder of Frank Olson and the CIA's secret Cold War experiments'. The book was published in 2009. Albarelli was shown some CIA documents whilst investigating the suspicious suicide of Frank Olson, a biochemist who worked for the Special Operations Division of the US Army. Olson had fallen from a window on the thirteenth floor of a New York hotel, two years after the incident in Pont-Saint-Esprit. According to the documents, this incident was the end result of an experiment undertaken as part of MKUltra, the CIA's notorious mind control programme. Former colleagues of Olson told Albarelli that Olson had been involved in the experiment and that the active agent was in fact LSD. The reader will have to decide for themself whether they believe that the events in Pont-Saint-Esprit were caused by the CIA or a criminal conspiracy between a farmer and a miller.

Morning glory

There are a number of plants that have the trivial name 'morning glory'. These include *Ipomoea tricolor* and *Turbina corymbosa* (synonym *Rivea corymbosa*). These plants have been used for centuries as entheogens by many Native American cultures, in what today we know as Mexico. The fact that they were used to generate spiritual experiences indicates that they have hallucinogenic potential. This was of great interest to the CIA who in 1956 studied their psychedelic potential in their MKUltra Subproject 22. By the mid-'60s the project was being wound down but whether deliberately or by chance, the San Francisco hippies got to hear about it. For a short time morning glory became a popular flower to grow, especially as it is a climber and needs little space. But what is the link to St. Anthony's Fire as alluded to at the beginning of the chapter? It has been known since 1960 that some morning glories produce ergot alkaloids. More recently, it has been discovered that these alkaloids are produced by fungi that infect the plants. These fungi are *Claviceps* species that are close relatives of the species causing ergot of rye.

PLANT PORTRAIT: MORNING GLORY

The plants known as morning glory (*Ipomoea tricolor* and *Turbina corymbosa*) belong to the family Convolvulaceae, the bindweed family. This is a family of about sixty genera and over sixteen hundred species. Most family members are herbaceous vines but there are some trees, shrubs and herbs. Particularly notable members are sweet potato and other food tubers. Members of the family are recognisable by their funnel-shaped, radially symmetrical corolla consisting of five sepals and five fused petals.

The plants known as morning glory are perennials that are native to the New World tropics but are widely cultivated elsewhere. In temperate climates they are grown in gardens as annuals or indoors as houseplants. Like all bindweeds, they grow as twining vines and can reach a height of seven to thirteen feet (two to four metres). Numerous cultivars have been selected for ornamental use and one, *Ipomoea tricolor* 'Heavenly Blue', has been given an Award of Garden Merit by the Royal Horticultural Society.

MISERY, MYSTERY and MAST

Tree species such as oak, beech and hickory produce nuts that are generally referred to as 'mast'. The term 'mast' is derived from an old English word 'mæst' meaning the nuts of forest trees that have accumulated on the ground, especially those nuts used to fatten domestic pigs. It was traditional to turn pigs loose into forests to fatten on this form of mast, a practice that continues today in those parts of Spain that produce jamón ibérica.

A mast year is when the trees that produce these fruits have a bumper crop and produce much more fruit than they normally would. Trees such as oak and beech fluctuate massively year on year in regards to the fruit they produce: some years no fruit will be seen and other years an exceptional crop is observed. It is believed that this is an evolutionary response to mast predation. Many animals including mammals and birds feed on this woodland fruit. In normal years, the trees produce little mast and this keeps these predator populations low. Then, during a mast year, more food is produced than these frugivores can possibly eat, ensuring that some seeds will start to grow. This has a major evolutionary advantage for the tree; producing seeds is costly work and therefore it needs to be ensured that some of their fruit will result in new trees. Producing fruit in a mast year does stunt growth of the tree but as this only occurs every five to ten years, it's a worthy pay off to ensure the production of more saplings. Unfortunately, mast years lead to increases in the mammals that feed on mast and this in turn leads to increases in human diseases.

Death at the Four Corners

The Four Corners is located in the Colorado Plateau desert region of the south-western United States. Its claim to fame is that the four states of Arizona, Colorado, New Mexico and Utah meet at a single point. There is no other place in the country where four states share a meeting point, leading the area to be known as the Four Corners region. This point also marks the boundary between two semi-autonomous Native American governments: the Navajo Nation and the Ute Mountain Ute Tribe. In 1993 it was to be the focus of a mysterious and deadly disease.

On May 14 1993, a nineteen-year-old man was rushed to hospital in New Mexico suffering from acute respiratory distress. The young man, a Navajo, was travelling in a car with his family on the way to the funeral of his fiancée when he was taken ill. The doctors were unable to save him and post-mortem X-rays revealed the reason: his lungs were filled with fluid. The death was particularly shocking because he had been physically fit and was a cross-country track star. Because his death was unexplained, medical reports and his body were passed to the Office of the Medical Investigator (OMI) for further review. There, the task fell to Richard Malone who was the deputy medical investigator. This was fortuitous because he was familiar with the Navajo community.

As soon as Malone picked up the case, he remembered that he had seen a similar case about one month earlier. A

Navajo woman aged thirty presented with mild flu-like symptoms and was dead a few days later. This was interesting, but when Malone questioned the young man's relatives, he realised he had a major problem. The fiancée whose funeral they had been going to had died five days earlier with similar symptoms. Malone had not known about this death because, unlike the other two, it had happened on Indian land and did not need to be reported to the OMI. By May 24 it was known that there had been at least seven cases of the mysterious flu-like illness in Navajos and six of the patients had died from respiratory distress. By the end of May more than a dozen new cases of the mysterious disease turned up and not all of them were among Navajos. The death rate remained high, even when the patients got to hospital fast, and death came quickly. One patient had breakfast in the morning, was on a respirator in the afternoon and was dead in the evening.

An intriguing aspect of the disease was that the lungs of all the patients were not filled with pus, as would have occurred if they had died from pneumonia, but with blood plasma. Even more puzzling was the finding that plasma tested negative for plague, which is endemic in the region, and for influenza, anthrax and Legionnaires' disease. Soon the Centers for Disease Control and Prevention (CDC) in Atlanta were involved. They drafted in a team from their Special Pathogens Branch, the créme de la créme of those who investigate infectious diseases. They routinely handle the deadliest microorganisms known to man, such as Marburg, Lassa and Ebola viruses. Within a few weeks they had identified the causative agent: it was a hantavirus. Later, the virus was given the name 'Sin Nombre', which sounds intimidating but simply is Spanish for 'without name'.

During the Korean War (1950-1953) there was an outbreak of haemorrhagic fever in the Hantan River area. The symptoms included bleeding of the kidneys and in some cases renal failure. More than three thousand troops were affected and there was a 10% mortality rate. This outbreak sparked a twenty-five-year search for the causative agent. This search ended in 1976 with the isolation of a new virus, Hantan virus, from the lungs of striped field mice. The disease that this virus causes is known as haemorrhagic fever with renal syndrome. Some two hundred thousand cases occur in Asia every year, about half of them in China. Outbreaks coincide with harvest times when farm workers disrupt rodent burrows, stirring up clouds of dust containing rodent urine as they do so. The disease starts with flu-like symptoms, progresses to internal haemorrhages, shock and failure of the kidneys. Once the Hantan virus had been isolated and studied in detail it was not long before close relatives of it, which have the generic name hantavirus, were found all over the world. In each case they caused mild forms of haemorrhagic fever with renal syndrome in patients that had been exposed to rodents.

It was not known why the disease caused by the hantavirus in the Four Corners region resulted in respiratory failure rather than renal failure, nor why it had such high mortality (~75%), but it was likely that rodents were involved. So, teams from the CDC began trapping rodents in and around homes of residents in the Four Corners region, including the homes of victims of the disease. Over a period of two months, more than one thousand nine hundred rodents were examined. About one third of them were carrying the virus and most were the common deer mouse. The virus causes no symptoms in the mice but is excreted in their urine. The mice are common inhabitants of dwellings in rural areas and humans probably get infected when they inhale urine-contaminated dust. The outbreak in the Four Corners region was at a time of year when many residents cleaned their sheds and other external buildings.

By now you might be wondering what all of the above has to do with plants. The answer is that the epidemiologists had to find an explanation for why the outbreak occurred when it did. The most likely one was that wet weather in the previous year had resulted in the yields of seeds, nuts and berries being up to ten times higher than normal, i.e. it had been a mast year. This in turn resulted in an explosion in the mouse population. When food is plentiful, a female can give birth to four or five litters of four pups in a single year. The pups themselves become fertile after two months and so you get a geometric increase in numbers. Crowding and competition between mice will lead to an increase in the proportion of animals carrying the Sin Nombre virus. As the countryside became overrun, people were more likely to encounter deer mice, and infected ones at that. But, there had been mast years many times before so why had there not been outbreaks before? The answer is that there probably were but if most of the deaths occurred on Indian reservations they would not have come to the attention of health authorities. Retrospective analysis of stored tissue samples uncovered a case where a thirty-eight-year-old resident died from Sin Nombre virus in 1959.

Gregory Glass, an epidemiologist at Johns Hopkins University, had been utilising satellite data to map animal populations. He realised that if he could map the distribution of animals, he could map the diseases that they carry. Consequently, the Four Corners disease outbreak was of great interest to him. He began reviewing satellite images from 1992, the year before the outbreak. It soon became clear that the 1991–92 El Niño had resulted in greatly increased rainfall and by late 1992 there was much more vegetation than normal. However, there was lush vegetation in many areas but no cases of Sin Nombre virus. Further examination of the data showed that all the cases of disease coincided with areas where there were lots of trees — the source of the mast. Where there was lush vegetation but few trees there was no disease.

Today, residents in areas where the disease is known to occur are encouraged to make their homes mouse-proof and to wear face masks or respirators if cleaning out-buildings. But that has not stopped cases of the disease occurring because scientists have developed specific diagnostic tests. As a result, many people previously diagnosed with respiratory distress syndrome have been found to be infected with a hantavirus, albeit not necessarily ones as lethal as the Sin Nombre virus.

The rise of Lyme disease

In 2016, former England rugby captain Matt Dawson was relaxing in a west London park when he was bitten by a tiny tick not much bigger than a poppy seed. By the time he was diagnosed with Lyme disease he had developed heart problems that required surgery. Dawson was lucky in that the correct diagnosis was made because he developed the characteristic 'bull's eye' rash at the site of the bite. Diagnosis needs to be made quickly for Lyme disease, also known as Lyme borreliosis, is a serious infectious disease. It is acquired following a bite from an *Ioxdes* tick that is infected with a bacterium known as *Borrelia*. Approximately 70–80% of infected people develop the 'bull's eye' rash and this is followed by flu-like symptoms such as fever, headaches and fatigue. If untreated, the symptoms can include repeated episodes of joint pain or heart palpitations. Even when patients are treated, they can experience long term effects such as loss of memory, neurological complications, or heart damage as in Dawson's case.

The natural host for the Lyme disease-causing *Borrelia* is mice who carry it in their blood without any effect on their health. When the eggs of *Ioxdes* ticks hatch, the larvae feed exclusively on mouse blood. There can be up to one hundred ticks on one mouse and the mice do not appear to mind the ticks' presence, because they do not remove them by grooming. As each tick ingests blood the *Borrelia* move to its gut and from there to the tick's saliva. If the next animal that the tick bites is uninfected then it will transmit the *Borrelia* to it. Ticks prefer to have a different host animal at each stage of their life cycle so as they develop into nymphs and then adults, they seek out animals such as deer as their source of blood. Humans are not their usual target: rather, they are inadvertent hosts, but that is of little consolation to those who get Lyme disease.

Rick Ostfield is an ecologist at the Cary Institute of Ecosystem Studies in Millbrook, New York. His wife, Felicia Keesing, is an ecologist at nearby Bard College. The duo are veterans of Lyme disease and tick research. Walking through the woods in the fall of 2015 they predicted an outbreak of Lyme disease in 2017. How did they know? Simply by looking at the number of acorns that littered the forest floor. It was a mast year. The abundance of acorns attracts white-tailed deer to the oak forests. In the autumn of mast years, the deer spend more than 40% of their time in oak stands compared with less than 5% in non-mast years. The mice also are attracted by the mast and so their numbers would be extremely high in 2016. As ticks feed on mice in their first year and only bite humans in their second year, 2017 was the year to worry about. Sure enough, the incidence of Lyme disease rocketed.

Lyme disease was first diagnosed as a separate condition in 1975 in Old Lyme, Connecticut. Prior to that it had been mistaken for juvenile rheumatoid arthritis. Recent statistics show that the numbers of people affected are about three hundred thousand per year in the United States and ninety thousand a year in Europe. The numbers of people affected are growing year on year. Why is this? The rise in reported numbers is partly due to improved diagnosis but mostly to increasing numbers of ticks. Oldfield attributes the latter observation to loss of biodiversity. As land is cleared for agriculture or housing there is a fragmentation of the ecosystem, which in turns reduces the numbers and diversity of animals that are present - animals that are not reservoirs of *Borrelia*. Instead, the numbers of mice and other potential hosts of *Borrelia*, such as chipmunks and shrews, increase in numbers leading to larger tick populations. Also, deer start to move into urban areas when land is cleared. This is of little consolation to Matt Dawson, as the park where he got bitten by the tick has a large resident population of deer.

A DUO OF DISAPPEARING DISEASES

What killed Abraham Lincoln's mother?

Nancy Hanks was twenty-two years old when she married Thomas Lincoln in 1806. Their union produced three children, one of which was Abraham who would go on to become the 16th President of the United States. The family had been living in Kentucky but in 1816 moved to Spencer County in Southern Indiana. There they set up home at Pigeon Creek Settlement. Two years later, Nancy Hanks Lincoln died of milk sickness at the age of thirty-four and became the most famous victim of the disease. Several relatives who lived nearby had died of the same disease just weeks before. Abraham helped his father to make his mother's coffin by whittling the wooden pegs that held the planks together. He was just nine years old.

Milk sickness was the leading cause of death and disability in communities in the Midwest and Upper South regions during the 18th and 19th centuries, as settlers spread westwards from the East Coast. It occurred most years and its effects were so devastating that many pioneers abandoned their new homes and turned about, greatly retarding the settlement of the west. The earliest cases of the disease were in North Carolina where a mountain peak was named Milk Sick. The term 'milk sickness' comes from the observation that the disease occurs in persons who have drunk raw milk from cattle suffering from a condition known as trembles. Affected cattle exhibit loss of appetite, stiffness, stumbling and trembling. In humans, the disease is characterised by a progressive acidosis that can kill within a few days to a few weeks. The condition is exacerbated by fatigue, poor nutrition and concurrent infection.

The incidence of milk sickness was greatest in dry years when cows wandered from drought-affected pastures into the woods in search of forage. Since the occurrence of the disease was restricted to late summer it had to be caused by something that the cows ate. That is, the disease was caused by poisoning, a conclusion supported by the fact that no fever was involved. But what was the offending plant?

In 1824, Anna Pierce and her family made a long journey in a covered wagon from Philadelphia to Rock Creek in south-eastern Illinois. There the family established a farm. Young Anna was disturbed by the poor health of the early pioneers like her family and vowed to do something about it. So, she returned to Philadelphia and took courses in nursing and midwifery, as medicine was not a profession open to women. After her training she returned to Rock Creek where she became the only health practitioner for a large part of the state. She became Anna Hobbs after she met and married Jefferson Hobbs who was a farmer and lay preacher.

To begin with, Anna Hobbs coped well with the ailments of her pioneer neighbours. Then the community was struck by an outbreak of disease where many people died despite her ministrations. The fatalities included her mother and sister-in-law and her father became seriously ill but survived with life-long disabilities. During the outbreak Anna had noted that all those affected had been drinking milk and eating butter: they had milk sickness. She must have been a good observer for she noted that although people were dying of the disease, the milk cows appeared not to be affected until after those that had drunk the milk had sickened. She wrote in her diary, 'I am convinced now that the poison which kills the calves and people saves the cows by being daily discharged through the milk glands. So I am writing a few letters this morning and telling everyone I can to abstain wholly from milk and butter from June till after killing frosts'.

Another observation that Anna Hobbs made was that horses, sheep and goats did not get the trembles, only cattle. From this she concluded that a plant was responsible for the disease. She noted in her diary that, "Sheep and goats are careful in selecting their foods, and horses are what teachers call graminivorous; that is, grass-eaters, while cattle are herbivorous and not careful in selecting. These things prove to us that it is not a grass, but an herb that is spreading sorrow and death among us." So, during the summer months she would follow the cattle and collect in her basket, samples of the plants that the cattle ate but, even so, she was not able to identify the culprit.

One day in the fall of 1834 Anna Hobbs set out as usual to follow the cattle to observe their feeding habits. About noon, she saw an Indian squaw hiding in the undergrowth and was delighted to find that she was a medicine woman who was a fugitive from a forced westward migration of Shawnees. Anna gave the starving Shawnee squaw her own lunch and took her home. Several days later, learning of Anna's interest in milk sickness, the squaw pointed out white snakeroot plants and said that they were the cause of trembles and milk sickness. She told Anna that the plant was well known to the Shawnee who used the root as a remedy for snakebite. Anna gathered a basket full of the white snakeroot and took it home where her husband fed it to a calf. Soon the animal developed the trembles. Anna started an ambitious snakeroot eradication programme and encouraged the local men and boys to search the locality for snakeroot and destroy it by burning. This programme continued for three years and after that the incidents of milk sickness in the community dropped to nil.

The detective work done by Anna Hobbs should have consigned milk sickness to history but it was not to be. Either she did not publicise enough her findings or else she was not believed by the medical fraternity because she was only a nurse. In 1838, a farmer from Ohio called John Rowe announced in a newspaper that he had discovered the cause of trembles in cattle. It was white snakeroot (*Eupatorium ageratoides*, now known as *Ageratina altissima*). He had killed some cattle by feeding them snakeroot and had also killed a pig by feeding it an extract of the plant. However, this finding was dismissed by other more eminent people who offered alternative explanations. Further evidence for the involvement of snakeroot came in 1867 after William Jerry ate some leaves, thinking that they would make excellent greens. A day later he became ill with violent trembling. He reported in the Missouri Republican that he had found the cause of milk sickness — but his claim also was ignored.

In the years that followed a number of other causes were put forward including microorganisms and arsenic. The latter explanation is not unreasonable as milk sickness and arsenic poisoning do have some symptoms in common. It was 1928 before snakeroot was definitively established as the cause. In that year, a number of poisonous substances were isolated from the plant and one of them was shown to cause the trembles. It was given the name tremetol but is in fact a mixture of substances. Later, in 1941, it was shown that the leaves were much more toxic than the stems. We now know that different wild varieties of snakeroot will produce different amounts of toxin and, within a variety, the amount produced will vary depending on the soil, the local environment and the weather. This might explain why for so long snakeroot was not accepted as the cause of milk sickness. A more likely explanation is that the physicians of the day were not trained in the scientific method — a skill inherent in Anna Hobbs! She was a very clever lady.

PLANT PORTRAIT: WHITE SNAKEROOT
(Ageratina altissima)

This member of the daisy family (*Asteraceae*) is a shade-loving plant found throughout Kentucky, Indiana, Illinois and western Ohio. It is not found on the East Coast of the US. This explains why it was unfamiliar to the early settlers in the Mid-West. The plants are self-supporting and can grow up to 1.5 metres tall. The flowers are a clean white colour and, after blooming, small seeds with fluffy white tails are released to blow in the wind. The generic name *Ageratina* is derived from Greek and means 'un-aging', a reference to the fact that the flowers keep their colour for a long time. The specific epithet *altissima* means 'the tallest', and probably indicates that this is the tallest species in its genus. A cultivar, sold under the name *Eupatorium rugosum* 'Chocolate' is grown as an ornamental plant because of its dark-tinted foliage. The darkest colour, which is chocolaty black, occurs in plants grown in a sunny location.

Cycads and flying foxes

Neurodegenerative diseases are incurable and debilitating conditions that result in progressive degeneration and/or death of the nerve cells (neurons) that are the building blocks of the brain and spinal cord. This degeneration causes problems with movement (ataxia) or mental functioning (dementia) as exemplified by conditions such as Parkinson's disease and Alzheimer's disease. The greatest risk factor for neurodegenerative diseases is ageing. Given that the average lifespan in Western countries increased by more than thirty years during the 20th century, it is easy to see why diseases like Alzheimer's have come to prominence in recent years. Most of us know someone with a neurodegenerative disease and worry that we ourselves might get one.

Scientists have had little success in developing treatments for neurodegenerative diseases and a major problem has been a clear understanding of the underlying cause or causes. When situations like this occur, and they occur often, scientists often turn to investigations of model systems of disease. That is, the examination of disease that occurs under special conditions that make it easy to study in the hope of finding clues that are generally applicable. The late Oliver Sacks was a distinguished neurobiologist who described just such a model system: Lytico-Bodig.

In 1996, Sacks wrote a book called 'The Island of the Colorblind' in which he told the story of the small Micronesian atoll of Pingelap where an unusually large proportion of the population is affected by complete colour blindness. It turns out that there is a very simple explanation for this but it is not relevant to our story. In the second part of the book, entitled

'Cycad Island', Sacks describes the Chamorro people of Guam who suffer from a neurodegenerative disease known locally as Lytico-Bodig disease. Between 1945 and 1956, this disease was the leading cause of adult death but showed a dramatic decline in the 1970s and 1980s. If a satisfactory explanation could be found for the decline then it could provide an understanding of the causes of neurodegeneration.

Although Lytico-Bodig are worded together, they actually represent two different diseases. The term 'lytico' comes from the Spanish word 'paralytico' which means weakness. 'Bodig' comes from the Spanish word 'bodega' meaning warehouse. It was the nickname of a man who owned a bodega in Saipan and who had symptoms of the disease when he returned to Guam. The onset of Lytico-Bodig typically occurred in people in their sixties or seventies with death following within five years. A genetic cause of Lytico-Bodig was ruled out even though it ran in families. Chamorro, who grew up outside of Guam, did not develop the disease and some people who moved to the island and followed the Chamorro culture did develop it.

An early hypothesis for the cause of Lytico-Bodig was a poison in the diet of affected people. Chamorros use a flour known as fadang to make foods such as flatbreads and dumplings. This fadang is made by grinding the seeds from a cycad (*Cycas micronesica*) that grows on Guam and some neighbouring islands. Before grinding, the seeds have to be soaked extensively and washed several times as the seeds in their native state are poisonous. They contain a potent toxin called cycasin. However, cycasin cannot be the cause of Lytico-Bodig as it is an acute poison that causes liver damage.

Cycad seeds contain another poison known as BMAA (beta-methylamino-L-alanine). Work in the 1980s showed that when this compound was fed to monkeys, they developed changes in their neurons. Could BMAA be the cause of Lytico-Bodig? The amount of BMAA in cycad fruit is about one gram per kilogram, so a monkey would have to be fed about forty-two kilograms of unwashed cycad for about three months to show neurone damage. Based on this, an adult human would need to consume 17.5 kilograms of unwashed cycad every day to show the effects seen in monkeys. This is unrealistic, so BMAA was dismissed as the causative agent.

In 2002, Sacks and American ethnobotanist Paul Alan Cox reignited the discussion on the role of BMAA in Lytico-Bodig. They suggested that the concentration of BMAA was magnified as it passed through the food chain. Later, Cox noted that tiny organisms known as cyanobacteria, or blue-green algae, can synthesise BMAA. These cyanobacteria exist in a symbiotic relationship with cycads and the BMAA that they produce gets transported to the cycad seeds. The concentration in the cycad seeds is over one hundred times greater than in the cyanobacteria that make it. Flying foxes, which are a kind of bat, feed on the cycad seeds and accumulate BMAA at even higher concentrations in all of their tissues.

The eating of flying foxes is a key component of Chamorro culture. Flying foxes are served at traditional feasts where they are prepared by boiling. They are eaten in their entirety: brains, viscera, fur and wing membranes. Humans cannot metabolise BMAA and so, if they do not excrete it, it will accumulate in their bodies until it reaches a toxic concentration. Supporting this idea is the finding of BMAA in the brains of Chamorros who died from Lytico-Bodig and in other people suffering from Alzheimer's disease.

If BMAA really is the cause of Lytico-Bodig, why did the disease reach a peak in the period 1945–1956 and then go into a steep decline? Consumption of flying foxes greatly increased after World War II as the Chamorros gained access to firearms and disposable incomes, as Guam was developed as a military base. Interviews with Chamorros indicated that flying foxes were a favoured food item and having a firearm made it easy to source them. Such was the consumption of flying foxes that the population of them has declined to a level where they are nearly extinct on the island. Another interesting observation is that Lytico-Bodig affected twice as many men as women. This could be explained by the fact that many Chamorro women do not like eating flying foxes because they think of them as flying rats.

It is fair to say that not everyone was convinced that BMAA accumulation was responsible for Lytico-Bodig in the Chamorro people. Nor, as it turns out, is Lytico-Bodig a good model for neurodegenerative diseases. Regardless, Cox continues to study the effects of BMAA on the brain and is investigating ways of minimising its deleterious effects on neurons. Other scientists are taking a fresh look at the role of BMAA in disease. Lotta Berntzon in Sweden has been monitoring the levels of BMAA in the Baltic Sea. Every so often there are blooms of blue-green algae and, just as in Guam, they produce BMAA. These algae are consumed by shellfish, such as mussels and oysters, and white fish. They too contain BMAA and the highest concentrations are found in the muscle and brains of bottom-dwelling fish. Given that BMAA is a neurotoxin, we shall have to wait and see if it is causing any neurodegenerative disease in people living around the Baltic Sea.

PLANT PORTRAIT: CYCADS

Cycads are seed plants with a long fossil history that were formerly more abundant and more diverse than they are today. They typically have a stout and woody trunk with a crown of large, hard and stiff, evergreen leaves. They usually have pinnate leaves. The individual plants are dioecious, i.e. they are either all male or all female. Cycads vary in size from having trunks only a few centimetres to several metres tall. They typically grow very slowly and live very long, with some specimens known to be as much as one thousand years old.

Cycads have a cylindrical trunk that usually does not branch. Leaves grow directly from the trunk and typically fall when older, to leave a crown of leaves at the top. The leaves grow in a rosette form, with new foliage emerging from the top and centre of the crown. The trunk may be buried, so the leaves appear to be emerging from the ground and the plant appears to be a basal rosette. The leaves are generally large in proportion to the trunk size, and sometimes even larger than the trunk.

Due to superficial similarities in foliage and plant structure between cycads and palms they are often confused with each other. In reality, they are completely unrelated and there are a number of key differences. Both male and female cycads bear a cone-like reproductive structure called a strobilus, while palms are flowering plants and bear fruit. The mature foliage looks very similar between both groups but there are key differences. The young emerging leaves of a cycad resemble a fiddlehead fern before they unfold and take their place in the rosette. By contrast, the leaves of palms are never coiled up and instead are just small versions of the mature frond.

KILLER PLANTS: NO THIRD-PARTY NEEDED

In 1999, Nicola Strickland and a friend took a holiday on the Caribbean island of Tobago. On their first day there they went to the beach and it was everything that they could have asked for: white sand, turquoise sea and swaying palms. While searching for exotic shells she saw some green fruits among the scattered coconuts and mangoes lying on the beach. The fruits looked like small, green apples and taking a bite from one she found it pleasantly sweet. At her suggestion, her friend also took a bite.

As a clinician, Strickland was able to describe clearly what happened next. Within minutes, she and her friend noticed a strange peppery feeling in their mouths. This gradually progressed to a burning, tearing sensation and tightness of the throat. The symptoms worsened over a couple of hours until they could barely swallow solid food because of the excruciating pain. As she wrote in a report in the British Medical Journal, "Sadly, the pain was exacerbated by most alcoholic beverages, although mildly appeased by pina coladas, but more so by milk alone". Over the next eight hours the oral symptoms abated but the two women had tenderness in their cervical lymph nodes.

What Nicola Strickland and her friend had encountered was the fruit of the machineel or beach apple (*Hippomane mancinella*). The Spanish-speaking locals call the tree 'la manzanilla de la muerte', literally 'little apple of death'. They stay well away from the tree and with good reason. In 1678 the Dutch writer Alexandre Exquemelin wrote a book entitled 'The Buccaneers of America'. In it he described a personal experience in Hispaniola with the machineel tree. He wrote, "One day being hugely tormented with mosquitoes or gnats, and as yet unacquainted with the nature of this tree, I cut a branch thereof to serve me instead of a fan, but all my face swelled the next day and filled with blisters, as if it were burnt to such a degree that I was blind for three days." A fellow sufferer was William Ellis, a surgeon's assistant on the third and final voyage of Captain James Cook. In 1776 he wrote in his journal, "… a party of men were sent to cut wood, as the island apparently afforded plenty; amongst other trees they unluckily cut down several of the machineel, the juice of which getting into their eyes, rendered them blind for several days."

The machineel tree is a member of the spurge family (Euphorbiaceae) and like other members of this family produces a milky, white sap. This contains phorbol and other light-sensitive skin irritants that can produce allergic contact dermatitis. Even standing beneath the tree during a rainstorm can result in blistering of the skin as toxic substances are washed off. Exquemelin, and the sailors accompanying William Ellis, were very lucky because getting the sap in the eyes can result in keratoconjunctivitis and permanent blindness. Not for nothing has the Guinness Book of Records given it the 'accolade' of the world's most dangerous tree. Should you be holidaying in the Caribbean you should stay well away from any tree marked with a red cross or with a painted red band around the trunk. But, be aware, not every country in the region gives visitors a warning.

A pair of pains: giant hogweed and poison ivy

Giant hogweed (*Heracleum mantegazzianum*) is native to the western Caucasus but was introduced to Britain as an ornamental plant in the early 19th century, because its impressive size made it a garden curiosity. It can grow to twenty feet with leaves spreading out like giant hands and flowers arranged in clusters the size of dinner plates. Within ten years the plant had escaped into the wild and by the middle of the 20th century was growing wild all over Western Europe. One hundred years after its introduction to Britain it was transported to the United States and Canada and here too it has gone wild and become a noxious weed. Unlike giant hogweed which is an introduced plant, poison ivy (*Toxicodendron radicans*) is native to the eastern half of North America. Despite its name, poison ivy is not a true ivy but is a relative of the trees that produce cashew and pistachio nuts. The species is variable in its appearance and habit, although it can grow as a vine it also is found as a shrub that can reach four feet in height.

As with the machineel tree, skin contact with giant hogweed and poison ivy results in an extremely painful and long-lasting dermatitis. The sap of giant hogweed contains compounds known as furocoumarins and these can be transferred to the skin simply by touching the roots, stems, leaves or flowers. When sunlight falls on contaminated skin it rapidly causes inflammation that is followed by severe blistering that can take months to heal and leave permanent scars. Years afterwards, the skin remains sensitive to sunlight. In the case of poison ivy, the toxic substance is a compound known as urushiol. About 15–25% of people have no reaction to contact with urushiol but at the other end of the spectrum, there are people who get anaphylaxis from it. Most people suffer from an itchy rash that can last anything from five to thirty days. However, the reaction is more severe with repeated exposure.

Poison ivy responds to increasing levels of carbon dioxide in the atmosphere by growing larger and producing more urushiol. In the last fifty years the growth and the potency of poison ivy has doubled. Urushiol has a long half-life and can remain active for years, even though the plant material containing it is long dead. If smoke from burning plants, dead or alive, is inhaled then a rash develops on the lining of the lungs causing extreme pain and even respiratory failure.

The delicious but deadly bunya bunya

The bunya bunya (*Araucaria bidwilli*) is a majestic Australian coniferous tree that is related to the monkey puzzle tree (*Araucaria araucana*). The tree has always been of great significance to indigenous Aboriginal people because of the seeds shed by the cones. These seeds are two to two and a half inches long by three quarters of an inch wide. They are sweet before being perfectly ripe and after that, resemble roasted chestnuts in taste. The seeds are only plentiful in occasional years (mast years) but in these years the local Aborigines would send out messengers to invite other tribes to come and sample the harvest. People would travel hundreds of miles to these bunya gatherings, which were covered by a tribal armistice and there would be much trade exchanged, discussions over marriage and settlement of differences. Sadly, the last of these was held around 1900 as European settlers began logging the trees for timber. Nevertheless, there still are some old trees that are marked with the hand and foot holes that Aborigines made in the trunks so that they could climb them to get the nuts before they were fully ripe.

So, what makes the bunya bunya deadly? The trees grow to a height of over one hundred and fifty feet and their branches have strings of very rigid and sharply pointed leaves. Unprotected physical contact with the leaves will result in deep cuts and severe pain. But that is nothing compared with the cones, they are up to twelve inches in diameter and weigh up to forty pounds! If one of these cones drops on your head then you are killed outright. Park your car under a tree with cones and when you come back you will think that some vandal has danced on it. There is a completely different tree in South America and India that is equally dangerous. This is the cannonball tree (*Couroupita guianensis*) which can grow to one hundred and thirty feet and produces hard fruits like a coconut that are ten inches in diameter.

Once stung, never forgotten

Australia has a reputation for being home to more things that want to kill you than any other civilised place on earth: bull sharks, box jellyfish, estuarine crocodiles, various snakes and funnel web spiders. Strangely, nobody talks about the venomous plants but they should at least tell you about the gympie gympie tree (*Dendrocnide moroides*) that is native to Queensland. It is known as the suicide tree for good reason.

Cyril Bromley was on a World War II training exercise when he fell into one of the trees. He ended up strapped into a hospital bed and described his condition as, "Mad as a cut snake". He also told of an officer who unknowingly used a leaf as makeshift toilet paper and ended up shooting himself. Ernie Rider was moving through the Queensland bush when he was slapped in the face, arms and chest by a gympie gympie. He said that it felt as if giant hands were trying to crush his chest. For three days the pain was unbearable and he could not work or sleep. He had severe pain for two weeks and for several years this pain returned every time that he had a shower.

The gympie gympie grows to a height of six feet and has heart-shaped leaves. Every part of the plant is covered in tiny, silica-tipped hairs that contain a toxin called moroidin. These hairs readily penetrate the skin and because they are so tiny the skin often closes over them making their removal near impossible. The pain comes immediately and is followed by erection of the skin hairs, arteriolar dilation and sweating. Because the stinging hairs are so fine, they can be broken off by the wind and inhaled by anyone in the vicinity. This results in long-lasting and very painful sneezing. There are other giant stinging nettles in other parts of the world, such as the giant Himalayan nettle (*Giardinia diversifolia*), but for causing long lasting agony none can match the gympie gympie. Maybe the spiders do not seem so bad after all!

PART THREE:
MURDER, MANSLAUGHTER
AND OTHER MISDEEDS

PEN PORTRAIT: AGATHA CHRISTIE, THE QUEEN OF POISONS

Aconite, which comes from the plants known as *Aconitum* or monkshood, is known as the queen of poisons. This is unfortunate, for the name really could be applied to Agatha Christie who is the most published novelist and was the doyen of crime writers. In the sixty-six murder mysteries that she wrote, more than thirty victims were killed by poisoning and other intended victims escaped the same fate. In her novel 'They do it with mirrors', she wrote, "Poison has a certain appeal, it has not the crudeness of the revolver bullet or the blunt instrument". What is interesting is that Christie almost always used real poisons in her stories and eschewed the use of untraceable or implausible ones. Her knowledge of poisons was extensive and one might ask how she acquired it.

Agatha Christie was born Agatha Mary Clarissa Miller in Torquay, Devon in September 1890. She described her childhood as 'very happy' and it was spent alternating between Devon, Ealing in West London where her aunt and step-grandmother lived, and holidaying in southern Europe. Her father died when she was eleven years old and she later claimed that this marked the end of her childhood. When she finished her schooling, latterly in Paris, her mother was ill and the two of them decided to spend time together in the warmer climate of Cairo. She also started searching for a husband. In

1913 she met an army officer, Archibald Christie, who had been seconded to the Royal Flying Corps. They married on Christmas Eve, 1914, while Archie was on home leave.

While Archie was off in France fighting the German forces, Christie was working as a volunteer nurse at a hospital in Torquay. Here she met many Belgian soldiers and refugees and they were the inspiration for her fictional detective, Hercule Poirot, a former Belgian police officer with a magnificent moustache and an egg-shaped head. He appeared in her first novel, 'The Mysterious Affair at Styles' which she wrote in 1916. When a new dispensary opened at the hospital, it was suggested that she might work there. To take on this new role she needed to pass examinations and become a qualified apothecary's assistant or dispenser. Up until the 1960s, when pre-packaged drugs became the norm, most medicines were assembled in the pharmacy from individual ingredients. It was a skilled job and called for a detailed knowledge of drugs.

Christie engaged a tutor to help her prepare for her apothecary's exams. She never identified this tutor, referring to him only as Mr P. One day he pulled a brown lump from his pocket and asked her what it might be. She had no idea. He explained that it was curare, a poison originally used on the tips of arrows by hunters in the Amazon basin. Wounded animals die because the poison gets into the bloodstream but the hunters can eat meat from the animals as the drug is inactive when ingested. Mr P explained that he carried it around with him because, "It makes me feel powerful". A character based on Mr P appears in her 1961 novel 'The Pale Horse'. In her autobiography she described how she came to develop the plots of her early novels: "Since I was surrounded by poison, perhaps it was natural that death by poisoning should be the method I selected". The plant poisons that feature in her novels include aconitine, atropine, the Calabar bean, digitalis, hemlock, nicotine, opium, ricin, strychnine and taxine — and all are described in this book. Christie's knowledge of poisons went far beyond what would be a lethal dose. She knew what the symptoms would be and the properties of the poisons. For example, taxine is too bitter to go undetected in tea but can be administered in marmalade!

In late 1926, Archie asked Agatha for a divorce. After a quarrel he left their house, aptly named 'Styles', to go and spend the weekend with his mistress. Agatha left a note for her secretary saying that she was going to Yorkshire. Later, her car was found perched above a quarry and containing some clothes. Her disappearance caused a public outcry. Sir Arthur Conan Doyle went so far as to give one of her gloves to a spirit medium to see if she could find out where Christie was. Eventually she was found staying in a hotel in Harrogate under a false name. The Christies divorced in 1928 but Agatha kept the surname for her writing.

After her divorce, Christie travelled on the Orient Express to Istanbul and later journeyed on to Baghdad. While on this trip she met a young archaeologist, Max Mallowan, who was thirteen years her junior. She married him in 1930 and they were happily married until her death in 1976. During the Second World War, Christie worked in the pharmacy at University College Hospital, London where she further refined her knowledge of poisons. The use of thallium as a poison was suggested to her by the Chief Pharmacist, Harold Davis, and this duly turned up in 'The Pale Horse'. Later, she was aghast when a factory worker called Graham Young used thallium to kill some of his co-workers in an exact copy of her story. It was the first time that this poison had knowingly been used in Britain. Later, in 1977, a French office worker called Roland Roussel murdered his aunt using atropine eye drops. The investigating officer found a copy of 'The Thirteen Problems' in Roussel's apartment (see p83). The pages describing the use of the poison were underlined!

Agatha Christie still is Torquay's best-known resident. Every September there are Agatha Christie events to celebrate the esteemed author's birthday and people travel from all over the world to mark the occasion. The town itself celebrates her achievements and knowledge of pharmacy with a Potent Plants Garden at Torre Abbey. Fans of the author can try to interpret the clues in the plant beds and solve the mystery of the missing story titles. Every plant in this garden feature appears in one or other of her stories or is connected in some way to her life.

THE POISONOUS POTATO FAMILY

In the late 15th century, the Portuguese ushered in the age of exploration. Christopher Columbus discovered the New World in 1492 and a few years later Vasco da Gama found a sea route to India. Over the next one hundred years, Europeans were introduced to a number of new plants that in the 21st century we consume with no thoughts as to their origins: potatoes, tomatoes, bell peppers, chilli peppers, aubergines (eggplant) and tobacco. One thing that all of these plants have in common is that they belong to the family Solanaceae, the nightshade or potato family. This is a very large plant family consisting of nearly one hundred genera and over two thousand seven hundred species. It has a worldwide distribution and many species, albeit ones not of economic importance, are native to Europe.

A key characteristic of all members of the potato family is that they produce chemicals known as alkaloids. For those with a familiarity with chemistry, alkaloids are a class of nitrogenous organic compounds of plant origin that have pronounced physiological actions on humans. The primary function of the alkaloids is to protect the plants from being eaten by insects and herbivores. This means that they are toxic. When we eat potatoes or tomatoes, we are eating the only parts of these plants that are not toxic.

There are four types of alkaloids found in the potato

family: solanine, capsaicinoids, nicotine and tropane alkaloids. Solanine is the principal alkaloid found in potato, tomato and aubergine plants. It is only of concern to humans if they eat green potatoes. When potato tubers are exposed to light, they turn green and increase their production of solanine. This is a natural defence to prevent the uncovered tuber from being eaten. Most people know not to eat potatoes that are green but in the 1970s there was a case of solanine poisoning affecting seventy-eight schoolboys in Britain.

Capsaicinoids are the active component of chilli peppers which are plants belonging to the genus *Capsicum*. They produce a burning sensation in any tissue with which they come in contact and the most potent capsaicinoid is the one known as capsaicin. It is commonly used in food products in the form of chilli powder or paprika to provide spiciness or 'heat' (piquancy). The burning and painful sensations associated with capsaicin result from its chemical interaction with sensory neurons. This has been turned to good use by applying it as an ointment or spray to relieve pain, particularly the excruciating neuropathic pain associated with shingles and cluster headaches. Other uses of capsaicin are the pepper sprays used by police for incapacitating violent offenders and to prevent rodents from eating electrical cables.

The notable case of nicotine and the nobleman

Nicotine is produced by plants belonging to the genus *Nicotiana*. A number of species of *Nicotiana* are grown as ornamental plants but the greatest use is for the production of tobacco. There is archaeological evidence of tobacco cultivation as early as 1200BC in what today is Mexico. The practice of smoking the leaves was brought to Europe from the Americas in the 16th century, a practice possibly learned from native North American Indians.

A single cigarette contains enough nicotine to kill a person if it were extracted and injected into them. However, no smoker dies of acute nicotine poisoning because of the way it is taken in and filtered in the lungs. Direct skin contact is a different matter and inexperienced pickers of leaves can develop an acute form of nicotine poisoning known as green tobacco sickness, particularly if the leaves are wet. There also is a new hazard and it comes from the use of e-cigarettes (vaping). A component of e-cigarettes is vaping liquid which effectively is a solution of nicotine. The inadvertent consumption of this liquid has led to tens of thousands of calls to poison centres and at least six deaths, of which two were in children.

There is only one recorded case of murder involving nicotine and that was in 1850. Count Bocarmé was a Belgian who inherited the family estate, Château de Bitremont, on the death of his father. He led an extravagant lifestyle and consequently was permanently short of money. So he married Lydie Fougnies, the daughter of a retired grocer, believing her to be rich. While she did have an income, it was not sufficient for their needs. Most of her father's fortune had gone to her unmarried brother, Gustave. He was not in good health and it was known that in the event of his death all his money would go to his sister. Imagine the Count's consternation when Gustave announced that he was getting married; he might change his will in favour of his new wife.

One night in late 1850, Gustave was invited to dinner at the château. It was an unusual occasion. The children usually ate their meals with the adults but on this occasion they had to eat in the kitchen. Stranger still, the meal was served by the Countess herself and not by the servants. At some point during the meal Gustave died and the servants were summoned to provide help with the body. They noted that the Count kept pouring vinegar down Gustave's throat. They also were puzzled when the Countess had all Gustave's clothes removed and washed in soapy water. The Countess then busied herself washing the floor of the dining room and later the Count was seen scraping it with a knife. The servants were very suspicious and decided to tell the local priest. Soon the local examining magistrate turned up at the château to investigate and on seeing Gustave's body was convinced of foul play.

Tissue samples from Gustave's body were put into alcohol and transported to the laboratory of Jean Stas, the foremost chemist in Belgium. Stas examined the body and was able to smell vinegar which led him to believe that this had been used to disguise the smell of the real poison. After much work, he extracted a substance from the stored tissue that smelled of nicotine. After even more work when he fed the substance to animals, he was able to prove that it was indeed nicotine. He also was able to extract nicotine from floor shavings indicating that there must have been a struggle with Gustave. A police search uncovered glassware used to prepare the nicotine as well as the corpses of several animals that had been used as test subjects. The gardener recalled the count purchasing a large quantity of tobacco leaves for the purpose of making 'perfume'. Finally, police enquiries resulted in several pharmacists coming forward to say that the Count had consulted them about extracting nicotine. The Count was convicted and executed but, amazingly, the Countess was found not guilty of any crime.

The success of many police investigations depends to a certain degree on luck and that certainly was the case with this case of nicotine poisoning. Most organic chemicals are soluble in either water or alcohol but not both. Alkaloids are an exception to this general rule. If you take body parts containing an alkaloid (nicotine) and add them to alcohol to which an acid (vinegar) has been added, the alkaloid will be extracted and can be isolated and purified. The Count's undoing was using vinegar to mask the smell of the nicotine used to poison Gustave.

So, why was this case notable? As stated earlier, it is the only known case of murder involving nicotine. However, it is notable for another reason. The work done by Jean Stas to extract and identify nicotine in the body and its environment at the time of death, led to a new methodology for crime scene investigation and for identifying alkaloids in forensic samples. This approach later was used successfully by another toxicologist in a case of poisoning with digitalis (p93).

The pharmaceutical poisons from the Old World

Most members of the Solanaceae produce the molecules known as tropane alkaloids. The most common of these tropane alkaloids are scopolamine, also known as hyoscine and atropine. Atropine gets its name from one of the plants that produces it, *Atropa belladonna*, otherwise known as deadly nightshade. The name Atropa comes from one of the three Greek Fates, Atropos, who would determine the course of a man's life by the weaving of threads that symbolised his birth, life and death. The job of Atropos was to cut these threads to end life. The specific epithet '*belladonna*' is derived from the Italian for 'pretty lady' and reflects the practice of women in earlier times of adding atropine to their eyes to enlarge their pupils to make themselves look more attractive.

The tropane alkaloids can be used to treat disease if applied at low doses but they are lethal if used at higher doses. This was well known to Pedanius Dioscorides, a first century physician who wrote a classic treatise, on plants as medicines, that still was being used in the 19th century. He knew which dose of atropine would cause hallucinations for days and which would kill a person, a useful attribute if you were a doctor in the Roman army. Given the ready availability of plants that produce atropine it is not surprising that it was a favourite poison in ancient Rome.

In the early part of the 1st century Livia, wife of Emperor Augustus, used atropine to murder her contemporaries. An even more accomplished poisoner with atropine was Locusta. She already was in prison on poisoning charges in AD54 when she was ordered by Agrippina the Younger to supply a poison for the murder of her husband Claudius. The next year she was called upon by Agrippina's son, the emperor Nero, to concoct a poison to murder Claudius's son Britannicus. Nero rewarded Locusta with a full pardon and an estate where he sent pupils to learn the craft of poisoning. Much later, in 1040, Macbeth is believed to have used atropine to murder an army of Danes during a truce. This was done on the orders of King Duncan.

Scopolamine gets its name from Scopolia, one of the plants that produces it. Its alternative name, hyoscine, is derived from another plant called *Hyoscyamus niger* or henbane. Among the known effects of scopolamine are sedation, confusion, disorientation and amnesia, and this possibly led to its use in flying ointment. If you were a witch and wanted to fly, you prepared an extract of henbane or similar plant, sometimes mixed with an extract of *Aconitum* (see p107). Rather than taking this by mouth, the extract was mixed with fat and smeared on a rod, such as a broomstick. When the witch sat on the broomstick there would be a rapid absorption of the drugs through the vaginal mucous membranes — and soon she would be off 'flying'. Some investigators in modern times have sought to recreate the flying ointment for their own use and lost their lives in the attempt. The historian and occultist Carl Kiesewetter of Meiningen was one such casualty.

Scopolamine is a key ingredient of the mandrake (*Mandragora sp.*), a plant that is common in the Mediterranean region. An extract of the root was used in Roman times as an aid to surgery for soldiers injured in battle. As Dioscorides said "The wine of the bark of the root is to be given to such as shall be cut or cauterised. They do not apprehend the pain because they are overborne with dead sleep." The clinical uses of mandrake were well known to William Shakespeare who used it no fewer than eight times in various plays such as Othello, Anthony and Cleopatra, and Romeo and Juliet (see p142).

Scopolamine began to enter mainstream medicine around 1880 and one of its first uses was in the induction of 'twilight sleep'. This is an amnesic condition characterised by insensitivity to pain without loss of consciousness and was induced by an injection of morphine and scopolamine. Its main use was to relieve the pain of childbirth or at least to create a state of amnesia so that the woman giving birth would not remember the pain. The use of this medication has been discontinued in favour of the gas Entonox, but both the mandrake and the opium poppy still adorn the coat of arms of the Royal College of Anaesthetists.

In 1922 it occurred to Robert House, an obstetrician from Dallas, that a form of twilight sleep could be used in the interrogation of suspected criminals. He gave scopolamine to two jail suspects whose guilt apparently was not in doubt. While under the influence of the drug both men denied the charges on which they were held and both men were found not guilty when their cases came to trial. Based on this success, House concluded that under the influence of scopolamine a person, "cannot create a lie… as there is no power to think or reason." Although House became an evangelist for the use of scopolamine in interrogations only a few police forces adopted it. One of the problems was that the side effects induced by the scopolamine led to hallucinations and it was not unknown for the suspects to talk gibberish. The idea of scopolamine re-surfaced during World War II when Nazi doctor Josef Mengele experimented with it as an aid to interrogation. In the 1950s both the CIA and the KGB also experimented with it as a 'truth serum', but they also found it to be useless.

Datura and the deadly dust

In 1676, settlers in the British colony of Virginia revolted against their Governor, Sir William Berkeley. British soldiers were sent to quell the rebellion and were quartered in Jamestown which was the first permanent settlement in the area. The soldiers were tricked into eating food laced with a local plant which subsequently got the name 'Jamestown weed' or 'jimsonweed'. The soldiers were rendered incapable of fighting for eleven days. Robert Beverley, in his 1705 book on the history of Virginia, described what had happened:

"…and some of them ate plentifully of it, the effect of which was a very pleasant comedy, for they turned natural fools upon it for several days: one would blow up a feather in the air; another would dart straws at it with much fury; and another, stark naked, was sitting up in a corner like a monkey, grinning and making mows [grimaces] at them; a fourth would fondly kiss and paw his companions, and sneer in their faces with a countenance more antic than any in a Dutch droll."

The above account is the first recorded poisoning with *Datura stramonium*. This is a showy member of the Solanaceae and all parts of the plant produce significant amounts of tropane alkaloids. The plant is native to North America but early explorers managed to spread it throughout the world's sub-tropical and temperate regions. *D. stramonium* has fragrant white or violet flowers that are trumpet-shaped and after pollination they produce egg-shaped seed capsules. At maturity, these capsules split into four chambers and each chamber produces dozens of small black seeds that are rich in scopolamine. Across the Americas, there is a history of the indigenous peoples ingesting these seeds to commune with deities and in Haiti they are an ingredient of the drinks voodoo priests use to create zombies.

Since the Jamestown incident there have been many reports of accidental and deliberate poisoning with *D. stramonium*. In the 18th and 19th centuries it was a popular murder weapon in North America and elsewhere, and today it still is used as such in India. The ability of scopolamine to induce amnesia, hence its use in 'twilight sleep', has made it a favourite weapon of criminals who use the seeds of *D.*

stramonium as a ready source of the drug. It has been used to trick women into prostitution, prostitutes have used it to rob clients, and in South America it frequently is used as a date-rape drug. In 2015, a French man died during a trip to Asia and an autopsy performed locally revealed no trauma, intoxication or pathology. A second autopsy was performed in France and scopolamine, atropine and hyoscyamine were found in the vitreous humour of the eye. Police investigators questioned the local travel guide in Asia who admitted having added *Datura* to a drink to stun and rob his victim.

In 2015, police in Paris arrested a group of Chinese who were believed to be part of an international Triad-style gang using scopolamine to rob victims of large sums of money. The group would approach strangers and blow a dust known as 'devil's breath' in their faces. This dust is powdered seeds of *D. stramonium* and is high in scopolamine. Victims recounted falling into a hypnotic state under the total sway of the criminals and giving them all their money and valuables such as jewellery. One person lost €100,000 (£73,000) in this way. When police raided the residence of the criminals in the seedy Saint-Denis district they found weighing scales, gloves and filters to facilitate handling of the 'devil's breath'. Examination of the criminals' passports showed that they had been operating in other European countries.

Some notable murders

Hawley Harvey Crippen qualified as a homeopathic doctor in his native US. In 1893 he met Clara Mackamotski, or Cora Turner as she called herself, in New York. After living in St. Louis for a period they moved to London in 1897 where Cora became a music hall entertainer with the stage name Belle Elmore. Some years later, Cora started an affair with a fellow entertainer and her relationship with Crippen became acrimonious. Crippen in turn developed a relationship with Ethel le Neve who was his secretary, or 'the typist' as Cora called her. For whatever reason, the Crippens did not do the sensible thing and get divorced. Instead, in 1910, Dr Crippen bought five grains of hyoscine hydrobromide (scopolamine) and poisoned his wife. He then cut her body into smaller parts and disposed of most of it. Failing to dispose of one of the bits later proved to be a significant mistake.

Cora's friends became concerned at her sudden disappearance and concern turned to suspicion when Ethel le Neve was seen living with Crippen and wearing some of Cora's jewellery. They reported this to the police who paid Crippen a visit. Crippen told Chief Inspector Walter Dew that he had received a letter from Cora saying that she had met someone else and returned to America. He also said that he had burned the letter. The police made a search of the house and after finding nothing they left, apparently satisfied. However, Crippen had been spooked by the police visit. He and Ethel fled to Belgium where they boarded the SS Montrose that was bound for Canada.

News of Crippen's sudden departure soon reached Scotland Yard and a more thorough search was made of the house. A torso was found under the brick floor of the basement and chemical analysis of the torso showed that it contained scopolamine. The media immediately reported that Crippen and his mistress were wanted for murder and this news even reached Captain Kendall of the SS Montrose. He was suspicious about two of his passengers and telegraphed the

British authorities. Inspector Dew boarded the much faster liner SS Laurentic in Liverpool and reached Canada before Crippen. As the SS Montrose entered the St Lawrence River, Dew came on board and arrested Crippen and Ethel le Neve.

Back in London, the fugitives went on trial. Crippen was found guilty of the murder of Cora and was hanged in Pentonville prison in November 1910. Le Neve was charged only with being an accessory after the fact and was acquitted. She emigrated to the United States on the morning of her lover's execution. The case became famous not just because of the story behind it but because it was the first one in which the new wireless telegraph system was used to catch a killer. It was immortalised in a popular song of the time:

> *Dr Crippen killed Belle Elmore*
> *Ran away with Miss le Neve*
> *Right across the ocean blue*
> *Followed by Inspector Dew*
> *Ship's ahoy, naughty boy!*

Whereas Crippen used scopolamine as his poison there have been a number of cases in which atropine was used as the murder weapon. On 24 December 1977 in Créances, France, Maxime Masseron and his wife sat down for their Christmas Eve meal. They had decided to open a bottle of Côtes du Rhône given to them in the summer by their nephew, Roland Roussel. The elderly couple were normally abstemious and they had saved the bottle for a special occasion. A few minutes after drinking some of the wine Maxime was dead and his wife was unconscious. Fortunately, a neighbour found the couple and Mrs Masseron was rushed to hospital but was still in a coma eleven days later. Doctors thought it was a case of food poisoning and that the couple had made a mistake in the preparation of their festive food. It was simply a tragic accident.

However, the diagnosis came into question a few days later when the couple's son-in-law and the local carpenter called at the Masseron's home to place Maxine's body in a coffin. The bottle of wine was still on the table and, deciding not to waste it, both men drank a glass. Within an hour both men collapsed on the floor unconscious but fortunately they survived. It was now clear that it wasn't food poisoning that had affected the Masserons and the police got involved. Analysis of the remaining wine revealed that it contained a lethal quantity of atropine. Roussel, who had presented the wine to the Masserons, immediately fell under suspicion and a police search of his apartment yielded some damning evidence. There was a bottle of atropine eyedrops, a magazine and newspaper articles on poisons, and a copy of Agatha Christie's book of short stories, 'The Thirteen Problems'. In one of these stories, 'The Thumb Mark of St. Peter', the victim was despatched with atropine - and Roussel had underlined the relevant parts of the story!

Another attempt at poisoning with atropine, this time in Scotland in 1994, was not as successful. Alexandra Agutter was drinking a gin and tonic but it did not taste right. It was too bitter and so she only drank some of it. Soon she felt ill. She became delirious, her vision blurred and her mouth became very dry. Her husband Paul Agutter, a biology professor at nearby Edinburgh Napier University, called their GP. There was no answer from the surgery and so he left a message. Alexandra's symptoms continued to worsen.

Fortunately for her, a locum practitioner had picked up Paul's message and alerted the emergency services. Finally, when paramedics arrived and Alexandra was taken to hospital, one of the ambulance technicians insisted on taking the rest of her gin and tonic for testing.

Alexandra's case generated national hysteria as seven other people in the Edinburgh area were hospitalised with the same symptoms. All had bought tonic water from the local supermarket and it was found to contain atropine. A young man named Wayne Smith then confessed to the crime of mass poisoning and at this point it seemed that the whole affair was down to an eccentric loner. However, analysis of Alexandra's gin and tonic showed that the concentration of atropine in her glass was higher than in the tonic bottles recovered from the supermarket. How could this be? The answer came from a worker in the supermarket where the contaminated bottles of tonic water had been found. He had seen a man putting bottles of tonic back on the shelves and CCTV cameras established that Paul Agutter was in the store at the time.

It transpired that Agutter wanted to kill his wife so that he could marry his mistress who was a student at his university. His choice of poison was atropine, something that he could buy as an academic researcher. However, his wife didn't drink the whole drink because it was so bitter and he had also miscalculated the amount which would be needed to kill her. He had doctored bottles of tonic water and put them back on the supermarket shelves as a smokescreen but made a critical error: he got the concentration of atropine in the bottles wrong. Alexandra Agutter still lives with the psychological scars of the attempted poisoning. And what of her ex-husband? After serving seven years in prison he was appointed as an ethics lecturer at Manchester University in 2003!

PLANT PORTRAIT: SOME DECORATIVE SOLANACEAE

The family Solanaceae comprises of about one hundred genera and these can take the form of herbs, shrubs, trees, vines and lianas. Apart from those used for food (potato, tomato, chilli and bell peppers and aubergines), a small number of genera are widely used as ornamental plants. These include *Petunia*, *Nicotiana*, *Datura* and *Brugmansia*. All of them have the characteristic flower structure

The garden petunia, *Petunia hybrida*, with its diversity of colour and morphology is the world's most popular bedding plant with an annual wholesale value exceeding $130 million in the US alone. The commercial *P. hybrida* is derived from crosses between a white-flowered, moth-pollinated *P. axillaris* and species of the *P. integrifolia* clade, a group of closely related bee-pollinated species and subspecies. The first hybrids were produced by European horticulturalists in the early nineteenth century and the remarkable phenotypic diversity in today's commercial garden petunias is the result of almost two centuries of intense commercial breeding.

The common horticultural forms of petunia are the Grandifloras, the Multifloras and the Surfinias. Grandiflora plants have a few, large, showy flowers on a stem. They are the best sellers but do not hold up well under adverse garden conditions. Multiflora petunias have more but smaller flowers on a stem and do better under garden conditions. Consequently, breeders have shifted emphasis to these forms. Surfinia plants were developed in Japan in the 1980s. They are trailing plants that are ideal for hanging baskets and are extremely vigorous and heat tolerant. In 2017, many petunia varieties were withdrawn from the market after it was discovered that they had been genetically-engineered and released without authorisation.

Nicotiana x sanderae, which is a cross between *N. alata* and *N. forgetiana*, is widely cultivated as an ornamental plant and is admired for its fragrance in the early evening. Being from warm, tropical and subtropical areas of North and South America, *Nicotiana* plants are classified as half-hardy annuals in Northern Europe and most of North America. They are also a popular cut flower and can be used in vegetable gardens to lure whitefly away from crops — the bugs get caught on the somewhat sticky leaves.

Two very decorative and closely-related members of the Solanaceae are *Datura* and *Brugmansia*. The former has a number of common names including devil's trumpets, moonflowers, jimsonweed and thorn-apple. The large, fragrant flowers on *Brugmansia* is the origin of their common name which is angel's trumpets. *Datura* species are herbaceous perennials with upward-facing flowers, whereas *Brugmansia* species are woody shrubs or small trees with pendulous flowers. These plants usually are grown in glasshouses except in sub-tropical areas.

DIGITALIS AND DEATH

George Eliot's novel 'Silas Marner: The Weaver of Raveloe', tells the story of a linen weaver who moves from the north of England to Raveloe in Warwickshire after being wrongly accused of theft. In the novel, Marner is taking a pair of shoes to be mended when he sees the cobbler's wife, Sally Oates, seated by the fire and suffering from the terrible symptoms of heart disease and dropsy. His mother had suffered from the same symptoms and had found great relief in taking a simple preparation of foxglove. Marner promises to bring Sally Oates something that will ease her plight. He finds some foxgloves, makes an appropriate preparation and administers it to her. Soon Sally Oates was feeling much better but, as word of her miraculous cure spread in the village, Marner was besieged with people wanting their various other diseases cured!

In the story of Silas Marner it is clear that Eliot had some knowledge of the discovery and medical use of foxglove by the physician William Withering. In 1776, Withering published 'The Botanical Arrangement of all the Vegetables Naturally Growing in Great Britain'. This was an early and influential British Flora. In it he mentions that foxgloves were used by herbalists and that this was worth investigating further. Over the next ten years he experimented with the plant using different dosage regimes in order to find the best way of administering it. In his classic paper of 1785, 'An Account of the Foxglove and Some of Its Medical Uses, with Practical Remarks on Dropsy and Other Diseases', Withering confessed to years of over-medicating patients to dangerous levels. This paper was notable in that it was the first documented report of a human clinical trial of a drug. In it he reported that over-dosing could result in nausea, vomiting, cardiac arrhythmias and even death. Vomiting probably hindered treatment and if the foxglove induced 'purging' (diarrhoea) it was sure to fail. However, when dosed correctly the results were remarkable as Withering wrote:

> *The foxglove's leaves with caution given*
> *Another proof of favouring Heaven*
> *Will happily display;*
> *The rapid pulse it can abate*
> *The hectic flush can moderate*
> *And, blest by Him whose will is fate*
> *May give a lengthened day.*

Withering was remarkable in another regard. He recognised the problems inherent in the use of plants as a source of medicines — something that many modern herbalists fail to do! The concentration of the active substance varies greatly depending on the species or variety that is used, the part(s) of the plant used and the time of harvesting. Withering chose to use only the leaves of the foxglove and to harvest them when the plant was in flower in an attempt to standardise the medicinal preparation. Not content with that, he would administer the extract in increasing doses until the first signs of side effects occurred and then stop treatment. Germane to this is an account of a near-fatal poisoning in which a woman stewed a large handful of foxglove leaves in a half pint of water and gave the liquid to her husband. As Withering wrote: "This good woman knew the medicine of her country, but not the dose of it, for the husband narrowly escaped with his life."

The active ingredient of foxglove was isolated one hundred years after Withering's landmark paper and, because the foxglove has the generic name *Digitalis*, was given the name digitoxin. The '-toxin' part of digitoxin is very appropriate for the drug has a very low therapeutic index, i.e. the ratio between a therapeutic and a toxic dose in some people can be a factor of only two. Much later, in 1930, a closely related compound called digoxin was isolated from *Digitalis lanata*. This now is the drug used clinically but it also has a very low therapeutic index. Since the metabolism of drugs slows down as people age, it is easy to give older people a lethal dose. This makes digoxin and digitoxin ideal murder weapons, something that did not escape the writers of crime fiction.

Fictional uses of digitoxin

The earliest fictional account of the use of foxglove as a murder weapon is the 1924 story of Precious Bane written by Mary Webb. This is the touching story of a girl living with an embittered brother and an ageing mother, on a small farm that barely gives them a living. The brother greatly resented the food that his invalid mother ate as well as her doctor's bills. Knowing that tolerance to digitalis decreases with increasing age he hastens his mother's demise by giving her tea containing digitalis. An interesting aspect of the story is that it is set in Shropshire where Webb grew up and where William

Withering first practised. Did this give her the idea for the story?

In Dorothy Sayers' 1928 novel 'The Unpleasantness at the Bellonna Club', an aged general dies shortly after receiving a very large inheritance in the will of his estranged sister. An argument over who should receive the general's money leads to the involvement of Sayers' fictional detective Lord Peter Wimsey. He orders an exhumation of the general's body and it is discovered that he has been poisoned with digitalis. The culprit is the general's doctor who was engaged to one of the beneficiaries if the general were to die.

Agatha Christie used poison as a murder weapon no fewer than eighty-three times and digitalis featured six times. In the 1938 story 'Appointment with Death', the Boynton family is on holiday in Jordan. On the first afternoon, all of the party except the malicious Mrs Boynton, visit the famous abandoned city of Petra. When the party return to their hotel, they find Mrs Boynton dead. The death would have been attributed to natural causes were it not for a mark left by a hypodermic syringe on Mrs Boynton's wrist(!) and some missing heart medicine. Of course, the inimitable Hercule Poirot is on holiday nearby and soon finds the murderer.

In Christie's the 'Postern of Fate' and the short story 'The Herb of Death', foxglove leaves are used to poison a meal by mixing them with sage and spinach leaves. One murderer deliberately planted foxgloves in a kitchen garden amongst the sage so that it would be picked by accident. A real-life accidental poisoning in 2016 mirrors these two stories. A 67-year-old Chinese woman in Vancouver presented to the emergency department with a three-day history of nausea, vomiting, heart palpitations and chest discomfort. Over the next few days, she exhibited various cardiac abnormalities. Then her husband was admitted with similar symptoms. Soon it was discovered that both of them had consumed a bitter-tasting leafy green plant. They had picked the leaves from their vegetable garden believing them to be kale. Blood analysis showed the presence of digoxin and the plants in their garden were found to be the foxglove.

Digitalis also found favour as a poison by American writers of crime fiction. In Elizabeth Peters' 'Die for Love', a gossip columnist dies what appears to be a natural death at a writers' convention in New York. A would-be writer is attending the convention and, as in all good crime stories, solves a crime that has baffled New York City Police. Digitalis turned up several times as the poison of choice in the TV drama 'Murder She Wrote', in which Angela Lansbury features as the sleuth Jessica Fletcher. In a major deviation from the original Ian Fleming script, James Bond nearly dies from cardiac arrest after his drink is spiked with digoxin in the 2006 movie Casino Royale. Thanks to the computerised clinical diagnostics system in his car (!) Bond quickly finds out what has poisoned him. A shot of lignocaine plus a jolt from a defibrillator and he is able to resume his fight against Britain's enemies. This treatment probably would have killed an ordinary person suffering from digoxin poisoning but we know that Bond is no ordinary person.

Real-life cases of poisoning with digitalis or digoxin

The first recorded case of poisoning with digitalis was in England in 1826 when a herbalist was accused of manslaughter, after his apprentice received a fatal dose. The herbalist was acquitted on the grounds that, "The act did not come under statute regarding manslaughter." In Ireland in 1851 a 'fairy doctress' was accused of killing a paralytic child with digitalis. Despite her plea that, "The child was stolen by fairies" she was found guilty. This prompted an article in the Edinburgh Medical and Surgical Journal entitled 'Deleterious practice of some of the Irish peasantry connected with the belief in fairies'. The first major case involving digitalis poisoning occurred in France in 1863 and has many features in common with some of the fictional murders described above.

Dr Edmond-Désiré Couty de la Pommerais convinced his mistress Madame Séraphine de Pauw to take part in an elaborate insurance swindle in order to pay off his debts. A number of large insurance policies were then taken out on Pauw's life. The plan was to then tell the insurance companies that Pauw had a terminal illness and would die soon. At this point the insurance companies would pay out an annuity until her death rather than a large sum upon her death. Pauw told her sister of the plan but was warned that Pommerais might kill her and keep all the money for himself. That indeed was what happened and Pommerais was convinced that he would not be found out because at that time there was not a definitive test for digitalis. The police were suspicious of Pauw's death and asked a respected toxicologist, Ambroise Tardieu, to search the body for signs of poison.

Tardieu was able to isolate a bitter-tasting substance but was unable to identify it. In desperation, he injected some into a healthy dog who soon began to vomit and exhibit signs of cardiac distress. When correspondence from Pommerais to Pauw was found that discussed the use of digitalis, Tardieu knew what he needed to do. He requested samples of Pauw's vomit but unfortunately none had been kept. So, the police collected samples from the floorboards where the vomit had dried and samples from the floorboards in other areas of the room. When the various samples were tested on frog hearts, the original substance extracted from Pauw's body and the vomit remains from the floorboards caused a significant reduction in heartbeat. Samples from the control floorboards produced no effect, thereby ruling out any possible effect of floor varnish or polish. This was a remarkable piece of forensic analysis given that it occurred over one hundred and fifty years ago. Just as in the Lindbergh case (p15), the defence lawyer tried to discredit the evidence but Pommerais was found guilty and was guillotined.

Over the next seventy years there were a number of other cases of deliberate poisoning with digitalis. In Germany, in 1876, two young men tried to get out of military service by getting an associate to give them the drug. One of the recruits died and the other recruit plus his associate went to prison for manslaughter. In 1930 in Belgium, a doctor poisoned the husband of his mistress by putting digitalis on the oysters he was served at dinner. Perhaps the strangest case of all occurred in Germany in 1934. An ear, nose and throat specialist wanted to get rid of his girlfriend but, rather than tell her the romance was over, he decided to kill her. Under the guise of conducting a medical examination of her, he placed digitoxin on his glove and administered the poison rectally. She survived long enough to tell the police that she was suspicious of her boyfriend's actions — perhaps the rectal examination by an ear nose and throat specialist alerted her. Regardless, she died and he was convicted of murder.

Digitoxin and digoxin featured as the poisons used by two mass murderers. The first of these was Marie Becker, a fifty-five-year-old Belgian housewife. Tiring of her husband, she poisoned him and obtained a substantial payment from a life insurance policy. She used this money to buy a dress shop that was supposed to fund her new and extravagant lifestyle. This included numerous love affairs with young men, some of whom were dispatched with digitoxin. She also poisoned her friends and collected bequests from their wills. She then started poisoning her customers: whilst they were examining dresses in her shop she would offer them tea laced with digitoxin. As soon as they died she would remove any cash and valuables on their persons. Nobody appeared to be suspicious about all the deaths occurring around Marie Becker.

The downfall of Marie Becker occurred when a friend complained to her about her husband and 'wished him dead'. Becker offered her friend a powder that would do the job and leave no trace. Instead of using the powder, the friend went to the police and Becker was arrested. The bodies of Becker's victims were exhumed and on examination were found to contain digitoxin. The fact that all of the victims had appeared to die from natural causes makes one wonder how many poisoners have used digitoxin and not been caught. Regardless, Becker was convicted on ten counts of murder although it is believed that the real number was twenty-five!

The most prolific serial killer in American history is Charles Edmund Cullen. In 1978, at the age of eighteen, he enlisted in the US Navy. After he rose to the rank of petty officer third class, he worked on a submarine where he was part of a team handling nuclear missiles. He attempted suicide on a number of occasions and was given a medical discharge from the Navy in 1984. Over the next sixteen years he had a career as a nurse in various hospitals in his home state of New Jersey. There were a number of unexplained deaths at hospitals where he worked but despite this, and his history of mental instability, he continued to find work. There was a national shortage of nurses and no reporting mechanism for nurses with mental health or employment problems.

In 2002, Cullen began working in the critical care unit of Somerset Medical Center in Somerville. Eventually the hospital's computer system flagged up that he was accessing the records of patients whom he was not nursing and also requesting medications that patients had not been prescribed. In July 2003, the New Jersey Poison Information and Education System warned Somerset hospital that at least four suspicious overdoses suggested that an employee was killing patients. When a patient died of low blood sugar in October 2003, the hospital called in the police. The hospital also fired Cullen. An investigation into his employment history revealed suspicions about his involvement with deaths in other hospitals.

Cullen was arrested in December 2003 and charged with one count of murder and one count of attempted murder. Over the ensuing months he admitted to more and more murders. He specifically remembered killing forty patients but there is evidence to suggest that the real number may be in the hundreds. Cullen used a number of drugs to poison his patients, including insulin, but digoxin was his favourite. When asked why he killed his patients he claimed that he wanted to end their suffering and stop hospital personnel from dehumanising them.

Two suspicious high-profile Italian deaths

Can Francesco della Scala, known as Cangrande, was the most famous member of the Scaligeri dynasty that ruled Verona for ninety years. He took the throne of Verona when he was just twenty years old. He gained a reputation as a warrior and a political leader and his rise to power was accompanied by the usual mix of intrigue, military conflicts and betrayal. But he was also a supporter of the arts and was a patron of the poet Dante. Throughout his reign he waged a campaign to take control of all of the northern cities in what is present-day Italy. In 1329 he reached his goal when he took control of Treviso. Four days later he was dead — at the age of thirty-eight.

Before he died, Cangrande had exhibited nausea, diarrhoea and fever. Some people thought that he had contracted dysentery which was not uncommon in these times. Others thought that he had been poisoned deliberately. Over the following centuries scholars debated the likely cause of death but there was no evidence to support any of the theories being discussed. Then, in 1923, archaeologists opened Cangrande's tomb and discovered that his body had mummified in the cold, dry air. But still there was no clue as to the cause of death. Decades later, in 2004, the city of Verona and the Castelvecchio Museum asked forensic pathologist Gino Fornaciari to examine the mummified body.

A mummified body contains no fluids so all Fornaciari had to work on was tissue samples taken from organs such as the intestines and the liver. A lucky find was the presence of faecal matter in the bowels that on microscopic examination revealed pollen grains from a species of *Digitalis*. Chemical analysis of the various tissues sampled revealed the presence of toxic concentrations of digoxin and digitoxin in the liver and faecal material — nearly seven hundred years after he had died. These results, coupled with the description of his symptoms prior to death, suggest that Cangrande died from poisoning with digitalis. Whether the poisoning was deliberate or accidental we will never know.

A more recent high-profile case, possibly involving digoxin, was the sudden death of Pope John Paul I in September 1978. His death fomented conspiracy theories that were the equal of the fictional works described earlier. The problem was that the Pope's reign of thirty-three days was one of the shortest in the annals of the papacy. Vatican Radio reported the death of 'the Smiling Pope':

"Today, on the morning of the 29th of September, at around 5.30, the Pope's private secretary entered the bedroom of his Holiness Pope John Paul I, as he had not found him in the chapel in the usual way. He found him dead on his bed and the light was still extinguished. The doctor who was immediately called in found that he had passed away at about 23 o'clock on the 28th of September."

However, there were discrepancies in the Vatican's account of the events surrounding the Pope's death. There were inaccurate statements about who had found him, and where, and what he had been reading at the time of his death. The undertakers who prepared his body for embalming claimed that it was still warm suggesting that he had died much later than claimed. The official cause of death was given as myocardial infarction but this came from a doctor who had never before examined the Pope. No autopsy was ordered to support the claimed cause of death.

The discrepancies in the details of the Pope's demise

fuelled speculation about a conspiracy of Masons, Mafiosi and Vatican bankers wanting him dead because he was going to expose their criminal activities. Within a few months, Abbé Georges de Nantes from the League of the Catholic Counter Reformation claimed that the Pope had been murdered. In 1983, Jean-Jacques Thierry produced a book that accused Cardinal Jean Villot of the murder. One year later, David Yallop claimed in his book 'In God's Name', that the Pope had been murdered because of corruption in the Vatican bank. Yallop claimed that the perpetrators included Cardinal Villot and Archbishop Paul Marcinkus who was the head of the Vatican bank, and that the cause of death was poisoning with digoxin.

Three years later, in an effort to stop the rumours of murder, Archbishop John Foley of the Pontifical Commission for Social Communications asked English journalist John Cornwell to investigate the issue. Cornwell is the brother of author and ex-spy John Le Carré so he should know something about investigation. He refuted Yallop's claims and, after consulting cardiologists and specialists in forensic medicine, decided that the Pope died from a pulmonary embolism.

What really caused the death of Pope John Paul? Without an exhumation and forensic examination of the body we will never know if he was poisoned with digoxin, as claimed by Yellen. Such an examination is unlikely in our lifetime but might not take seven hundred years as it did for Cangrande.

PLANT PORTRAIT: THE FOXGLOVE (*Digitalis sp.*)

Digitalis is a genus of about twenty species of herbaceous biennials and perennials, known commonly as foxgloves, plus a few shrubs. The scientific name means 'finger like' and refers to the ease with which a flower of the common European foxglove, *Digitalis purpurea*, can be fitted over a human fingertip. The name 'foxglove' was first recorded in 1542 by the botanist Leonhard Fuchs. His family name, Fuchs, is the German word for fox.

There are many attractive colour forms of *D. purpurea* that are garden worthy but this species is a biennial, and only flowers in its second year. Other readily-available species are *D. lutea, D. grandiflora, D. ferruginea, D. parviflora* and *D. lanata*. The first two have quite insipid, yellow-coloured flowers and a tendency to self-seed. The other three have much more interesting flowers and are worthy of a place in the garden. Recently, breeders have been crossing *Digitalis purpurea* with *Isoplexus sp.* (the Canary Island foxglove) to create hybrids such as *Digitalis* Illumination Pink. These hybrids have very attractive colouring but are not hardy in much of the UK.

All parts of foxgloves are poisonous because they make compounds such as digitoxin and digoxin. The main source of digoxin for pharmaceutical use is high- yielding strains of *D. lanata*. During World War II there was a shortage of digoxin and so digitoxin was produced from the common foxglove *D. purpurea*. The plants were collected by members of the Women's Institute around Oxfordshire and neighbouring counties and supplied to a processing plant at Islip near Oxford.

The suicide or murder tree

Cerbera odollum is a medium-sized hardwood tree endemic to India and South-East Asia that is a close relative of oleander. It produces a fruit that looks like a small green mango and inside of this is a kernel. This kernel contains a compound called cerberin that chemically is very similar to digoxin. Ingesting one seed from a *Cerbera* plant will result in death within a few hours but first it will cause crippling stomach pain, diarrhoea, irregular heart rhythm, vomiting and a headache. A lady in the US who suffered from depression purchased several seeds on-line and ingested them. Soon she was rushed to hospital and as her clinical signs resembled digoxin poisoning. They administered an anti-digoxin antibody. This saved her life but only because cerberin is structurally very like digoxin.

The tree gets its gruesome moniker 'the suicide tree' from the fact that toxicologists believe that it is used to commit suicide by more people than any other plant on earth. In a ten-year period from 1989 to 1999 there were five hundred and thirty-seven deaths caused by cerberin in the Indian state of Kerala alone. The lethality of cerberin is well known and most of the deaths resulted from deliberate ingestion: individuals remove the kernel from the fibrous seed husk, mash it with cane sugar to cover the bitterness and then eat it. The Indian authorities are not sure how often cerberin is used to commit murder, particularly in rural areas where there are no analytical laboratories. All that is required to kill someone is to add mashed kernel to some spicy food.

Oleander: the suicide bush and fabled poison weapon

There are two closely related plants, which are known as oleanders. *Nerium oleander*, commonly known as 'oleander', is so widely cultivated that no precise region of origin has been identified. *Cascabela thevetia* (*Thevetia peruviana*) is native to Mexico and Central America but it is grown widely elsewhere including the US, southern India and Sri Lanka. These two plants are in a different family (Apocyanaceae) from the foxglove (Lamiaceae) but have something in common with it: they produce cardiac glycosides with a narrow therapeutic index. The similarity is so great that antibodies used to treat digoxin poisoning also can be used to treat oleander poisoning.

There is an urban myth about the toxicity of oleanders that is repeated in various forms around the world. In one version, some of Wellington's soldiers in the Peninsular War died after eating meat cooked on skewers made from the wood. In other versions of the story it was Napoleon's or Alexander the Great's soldiers or even boy scouts out camping. Soldiers sleeping on oleander branches were reported to have died according to an 1880 edition of the Gardener's Chronicle but this probably is another version of the skewer story.

There are a number of unsubstantiated stories about oleander being used deliberately to poison people. Nearly two hundred years ago, Judge Clark Woodruffe owned the Myrtles Plantation in St Francisville, Louisiana. He had a slave girl, Chloe, who cleaned and cooked for him, his wife and three children. The judge took her as an unwilling mistress and then lost interest in her. Fearing she would be sent to work in the field with the other slaves, she devised a plan to poison a birthday cake with oleander leaves. She then would prove her worth by nursing the recipients back to health. Her plan failed. Mrs Woodruffe and two of the daughters died of oleander poisoning. Chloe fled the plantation house but was caught by the other slaves and hanged. This story is plausible but it is not true. The reality is that the victims died from yellow fever.

Another fable about oleander poisoning is the story of Lavinia Fisher who in the early 1800s kept an inn known as the Six Mile House on the road from Georgia to Charleston. Newly arrived guests would be questioned discreetly about their finances. If they appeared to be wealthy, then they would be offered a cup of tea made with oleander leaves. After the victim died, their body would be stripped of valuables before being buried. However, poisoning with oleander tea is not entirely fictitious. In 2003, Angelina Rodriguez was sentenced to death for the murder of her fourth husband. Soon after marrying him in April 2000 she took out a life insurance policy with a value of $250,000. Her husband died in September of that year but the cause of death was undetermined. This meant that the life insurance company would not pay out on the policy. Angelina asked for more tests to be done and these revealed that her husband had been poisoned. It transpired that she had used both oleander tea and Gatoraid laced with anti-freeze. In a similar case in Australia, a woman fed her husband oleander tea because he was a 'lousy lover'. He survived and she went to jail. In Italy, a couple were admitted to hospital with symptoms typical of acute digoxin ingestion. The couple had eaten a meal that included snail stew and the analysis of some leftover snails identified the presence of oleandrin.

The yellow oleander has trumpet-like flowers and a fruit

the size of a chestnut. Inside the fruit is a single large seed and ingestion of this is sufficient to cause death. The fatality rate is about 10% but would be lower if the anti-digoxin antibody was affordable. Because of the widespread distribution of the yellow oleander in Sri Lanka, it is easy for a person wishing to commit suicide to get access to the seeds. Strangely, attempted suicide with yellow oleander is only common in Sri Lanka, despite the plant growing widely in the tropics, and the incidence has been rising since the turn of the century.

POISONS ANCIENT AND MODERN

Ask anyone to name a plant poison and there is a high probability that the first one that they think of is hemlock (*Conium maculatum*). This is strange because the last known case of deliberate poisoning with this plant was in Ancient Greece where it was used regularly to execute condemned prisoners. The most famous of these was Socrates in 399 BC but other notable deaths from that period were Theramenes (404 BC) and Phocion (318 BC). It is not clear why hemlock has not featured as a murder weapon in modern times for the plant is easy to find. It is native to Europe and North Africa but has been naturalised in other areas including Asia, North America, Australia and New Zealand. A related plant, water dropwort (*Oenanthe crocata*), is the most poisonous indigenous plant in Britain.

Although hemlock and water dropwort have not been used for murder they feature regularly in reports of accidental poisoning. There is a reason for this. Both plants belong to the Apiaceae or umbellifer family to which parsley, celery, parsnip and carrots also belong. Most of those who have been poisoned ate the hemlock or water dropwort thinking they were one of the more familiar vegetables. This happened in 2020 when a French survival course leader was charged with manslaughter after telling a course participant that a hemlock plant, was a harmless wild carrot. There also have been cases of indirect poisoning called coturnism. These occur in the Mediterranean region when people eat wild birds such as quails (*Coturnix coturnix*) that have fed on hemlock. The birds are immune to the poison, coniine, present in the plants but it concentrates in their tissues and is not completely destroyed by subsequent cooking.

We know quite a lot about the effects of consumption of hemlock from the contemporary descriptions of the death of Socrates by Plato and others. Socrates had been charged with 'refusing to recognise the gods recognised by the state' and of 'corrupting the youth'. After hearing the arguments of both Socrates and his accusers, the jury of five hundred Athenians found him guilty by a majority vote (two hundred and eighty out of five hundred). His accusers argued for the death penalty and Socrates was given the opportunity to suggest his own punishment. Had he suggested exile he could have avoided execution but instead he mocked his accusers. Athenian law prescribed death by drinking a cup of hemlock.

Plato's fictional character Phaedo describes the execution. After the sentence was passed, a slave boy went out of the court and brought in the man who was to administer the poison. The hemlock was already prepared as a drink. Socrates asked the executioner what he should do. The response was, "Just drink it and walk around until your legs begin to feel heavy, then lie down. It soon will act." Socrates walked around until he said that his legs were becoming heavy and then he lay on his back as the executioner instructed. The executioner felt him and then a moment later examined his feet and legs again. Squeezing a foot hard he asked Socrates if he felt anything. Socrates said that he did not. The executioner then squeezed the calves of Socrates and when these were stiff, moved up to the thighs. When the chill reached the region about the groin, Socrates uncovered his face, which up until this time had been covered. He said, "Crito, we owe a cock to Asclepius. Do pay it and do not neglect it." These were his last words.

Plato gives a good description of the effects of coniine on the body. A Scottish physician, John Harley, tested poison hemlock on himself in the 19th century and his description of the effects agrees rather well with that of Socrates'. It disrupts the peripheral nervous system and causes ascending paralysis. This is what the executioner of Socrates was monitoring. Death comes from respiratory paralysis following failure of the heart. A 19th century American doctor reported the case of someone who had eaten a large quantity of hemlock mistaking it for parsley. The patient soon lost the feeling in his legs but it was over three hours before he died of respiratory failure. Like Socrates, he was alert until his death. It could be said that Socrates was lucky in having a competent executioner. When Phocion was condemned to death in 318 BC, the dose of hemlock provided proved insufficient to be lethal. The executioner refused to prepare more unless he was paid twelve drachmas. Phocion remarked, "In Athens, it is hard for a man even to die without paying for it." A friend paid the executioner the extra sum on his behalf and Phocion drank his poison and died.

Aconite and the 'Curry Killer'

Another poisonous plant well known to the ancient Greeks is *Aconitum variegatum*. It featured in Greek mythology when the goddess Hecate invented aconite that Athena then used to transform Arachne into a spider. The plant has the common names wolf's bane, leopard's bane, monkshood and queen of poisons. The scientific name derives from the Greek 'akon' meaning dart or javelin, the tips of which were coated with the juice of the plant to kill wolves. This is the origin of the common name 'wolf's bane'. The flowers are not symmetrical and have the appearance of a helmet or hood hence the common English name 'monkshood'.

In his mythological poem 'Metamorphoses', Ovid tells how *Aconitum* comes from the slavering mouth of Cerberus, the three-headed dog that guarded the gates of Hades. Hercules was challenged to bring the hell-bound from the Underworld to the surface and this necessitated wrestling with the beast. As he did so, saliva from Cerberus' three mouths dripped on the ground and where this happened poisonous flowers grew. The symptoms of aconite poisoning in humans bear some passing similarity to those of rabies: frothy saliva, impaired vision, vertigo, and finally coma. Thus the ancient Greeks may have believed that this poison, mythically born of the lips of Cerberus, was literally the same as that found inside the mouth of a rabid dog.

Brigadier-General John Nicholson (1821 – 1857) was a Victorian era military officer known for his role in British India. He is famous for leading the storming of Delhi during the Indian Mutiny. One night during this campaign he strode into the mess tent at Jullunder, coughed to attract the attention of the officers, and said, "I am sorry, gentlemen, to have kept you waiting for your dinner, but I have been hanging your cooks." He had been told that the regimental chefs had poisoned the soup with aconite. When they refused to taste it for him, he force-fed it to a monkey. The monkey died almost immediately and he proceeded to hang the cooks from a nearby tree without giving them a trial.

Brighton on the south coast of England was the scene of a possible multiple murder with aconite. Helen Warder was murdered by her husband, Alfred, a doctor who administered aconite to her over a period of one month. Her brother was a local surgeon, and as his sister's condition deteriorated, he suspected that her husband was not dispensing to her the correct medicines to remedy the mysterious illness. When Mrs. Warder died another doctor considered the circumstances to be so irregular that he refused to sign the death certificate. Consequently, a coroner's inquest was constituted. Her widower husband went off to London but returned discreetly and booked himself into a local hotel where he committed suicide by drinking prussic acid. Staff found his naked body in bed the following morning. It transpired that he had married twice before and each of his wives had died in unnatural circumstances.

Another famous case of aconite poisoning in Victorian England involved Dr George Henry Lamson. He was an American doctor who had fought during the Franco-Prussian War with the French Ambulance Corps during the 1871 siege of Paris. For this he was awarded the Légion d'honneur. He settled in Bournemouth as a GP but had developed an addiction to morphine, possibly as a result of his experiences of war. This addiction caused financial difficulties and he decided to murder one of his wife's brothers, Percy, to get access to his inheritance. He chose aconitine as the murder weapon and purchased some from a pharmacist in London. The pharmacist asked Lamson for his name and, because he was listed in the register of medical professionals, sold it to him without question.

It is not clear how the aconitine was administered to Percy but its effects were devastating. He convulsed so violently that he had to be forcible restrained. His mouth and throat were burning and he said that he felt as if his skin was being pulled from him. Percy eventually died after four hours of torment. Poisoning was suspected and a toxicologist, Dr Thomas Stevenson, was asked to investigate. He managed to extract a substance from Percy's organs but was unable to identify it chemically. However, he was an expert in alkaloid poisons and he had a party trick: he could identify over fifty alkaloids by taste alone. Stevenson claimed that the taste and burning sensations of aconitine were unique and concluded that this poison had been administered to Percy.

Lamson had been taught in medical school that acontine was undetectable because there was no chemical test and this probably was why he had chosen it to murder Percy. However, his misfortune was that Stevenson, the toxicologist with the unique palette for poisons, was called in by the police. When the case came to trial at the Old Bailey it made headlines in the newspapers and the pharmacist who had sold Lamson the aconitine came forward to testify. Lamson was sentenced to death. His execution was delayed when word came that his friends and family in the United States, including President Chester Arthur, requested time to send proof of insanity in the doctor's family and in his own life. The evidence was sent but was not sufficient to reduce the sentence. He was hanged in Wandsworth Prison in April 1882.

Aconite as a murder weapon reared its head again in 2007 when Bob Woolmer died in suspicious circumstances. Woolmer was a professional cricketer who played for Kent and then graduated to Test cricket with England in 1975. After retiring from first-class cricket in 1984 he became a professional coach of the game. At the time of his death he was coaching the Pakistan team. On 18 March 2007, Woolmer died suddenly in Jamaica, just a few hours after the Pakistan team's unexpected elimination at the hands of Ireland in the 2007 Cricket World Cup. The initial cause of death was said to be a heart attack but an anonymous man phoned police to say that Woolmer had been killed with aconite. This was a time when Asian gambling syndicates were paying players to lose matches and players who did not succumb to bribes could be murdered. After a long investigation which most people believe was bungled, not deliberately but through incompetence, it was concluded that Woolmer had indeed died of natural causes. A number of professional cricketers from that period, such as former Australian captain Ian Chappell, still believe that Woolmer was murdered.

The year after Woolmer died aconite was back in the news and this time there was no doubt that it had been used to murder someone. After his first marriage failed, Lakhvinder Cheema began what was to be a sixteen-year affair with an older, married woman called Lakhvir Singh. In October 2008 Cheema told Singh that he was ending their affair as he planned to marry a younger woman. Shortly before this, Singh had threatened to burn down Cheema's house after finding him in bed with his new amour. After the break-up of the affair, Cheema was hospitalised with suspected poisoning after consuming a meal prepared by Singh. Meanwhile, Singh went on a trip to India, ostensibly to get over the affair.

A variety of *Aconitum* called *A. ferox* grows in the Himalayas. It contains large quantities of the alkaloid known as pseudaconitine and the Nepalese use it as a poison called variously bikh, bish or nabee. When Singh returned to England she brought some of this material with her. She still had a key to Cheema's house so she went there armed with the poison and laced a curry that she found in the refrigerator. That evening, Cheema and his fiancée ate the curry and soon became very sick. Cheema dialled 999 and told the emergency operator that he had been poisoned. A few hours later he died but not before describing his symptoms as being like having ants crawl all over him. These sounded similar to the ones reported by Lamson's victim Percy over one hundred years before. Cheema's fiancée suffered the same symptoms but survived, after being put into a medically-induced coma until the effects of the drug wore off.

Suspicion for Cheema's death soon fell on Singh. She tried to blame her brother-in-law for the crime but a lodger in Cheema's house had seen Singh taking the curry out of the refrigerator on the day of the murder. Police also found in Singh's possession, a plastic bag containing a brown powder. On analysis, this was found to contain pseudaconitine and matched the poison found in the curry. Dubbed 'The Curry Killer' by the British press, Singh was found guilty after a trial at the Old Bailey and sentenced to life in prison.

PLANT PORTRAIT: *Aconitum*

Aconitum species are widely cultivated as garden plants although most of the ones available from plant centres are modern hybrid varieties. They have several attributes that make them garden worthy: they are long-lived perennials that require little attention, they flower in late summer when many other perennials have stopped flowering and they are not fussy about growing conditions and will thrive even under trees. There also are a few climbing varieties such as *A. hemsleyanum*. The typical flower colour is dark blue-purple but the newer hybrids can be white, greenish-yellow or even bicoloured. The Royal Horticultural Society has given an Award of Garden Merit (AGM) to four varieties: *A. x cammarum* 'Bicolour', 'Bressingham Spire' bred by the late Alan Bloom, 'Spark's Variety' developed in 1897 in Christchurch in Hampshire and 'Stainless Steel' with steely blue flowers. If bare hands come in contact with the juice from cut stems then the result can be temporary numbness of the fingers so the wearing of gloves is recommended.

Did Jack the Ripper also use strychnine?

Whereas hemlock and aconite were used as poisons in ancient Greece and in the Roman Empire, strychnine is a relatively new poison. This is because the strychnine tree (*Strychnos nux-vomica*) is native to India and south-east Asia and its poison did not reach Europe until after the Age of Exploration. The specific name 'nux-vomica' literally means 'the nut that makes you vomit' and indicates the historical use of strychnine as an emetic. There is only a small difference between a therapeutic dose and a lethal dose of strychnine and death can occur following inhalation, ingestion or absorption through the eyes or mouth. A lethal dose will cause death in two to three hours and will produce the most dramatic and painful symptoms of any poison. These include extreme sensitivity to sensory stimuli and convulsions that cause the spine to bend back. Jane Stanford, co-founder of Stanford University and wife of California governor Leland Stanford, died from strychnine poisoning in 1905. Her last recorded words were "My jaws are stiff. This is a horrible death to die." Her killer was never identified.

The first person in Britain to be convicted of murder by strychnine poisoning was William Palmer. His crime was one of the most notorious cases of murder in the 19th century and Charles Dickens called him the greatest villain that ever stood in the dock at the Old Bailey. Palmer qualified in London as a doctor and established himself as a GP in his native Staffordshire. Shortly afterwards he met a man called George Abley in a pub and challenged him to a drinking contest. Abley accepted and one hour later he was carried home where he died in bed. Foul play was not suspected but locals noted Palmer's interest in Abley's attractive wife. The following year Palmer got married to a lady whose mother supposedly had inherited a fortune. Eighteen months later the mother came to stay with Palmer and two weeks after arriving she died of 'apoplexy'. Palmer was 'disappointed' with the inheritance that his wife received.

Palmer became interested in horse-racing and began betting heavily but with little success. Soon he was heavily in debt. One man died in agony in Palmer's house shortly after having lent Palmer money. In 1854, Palmer took out a life insurance policy on his wife for the sum of £13,000 and six months later she was dead. She was only twenty-seven years of age and was believed to have died of cholera as there was a cholera epidemic in England at the time. It is worth noting that four out of five of the Palmer's children had died in infancy. These were not thought to be suspicious as infant mortality was common at the time even though such mortality was heavily biased to working class children.

The year after his wife's death, Palmer took out an insurance policy on his brother Walter for the sum of £14,000. Walter died soon afterwards but the insurance company refused to pay up and ordered an enquiry into his death. By now Palmer was desperate for money because he was heavily in debt and his creditors were exerting a lot of pressure. He had a friend called John Cook who was wealthy and, like him, interested in horseracing. Whereas Cook had a habit of picking winners, and even won £3,000 on one race, Palmer kept backing losers. Cook started experiencing bouts of vomiting over a period of a few weeks and then died in agony screaming that he was suffocating — characteristic symptoms of strychnine poisoning. Palmer obtained a death certificate from a fellow doctor who recorded the cause of death as apoplexy.

Cook's relatives were suspicious about the cause of his death, particularly as there appeared to be irregularities in his financial affairs. A post-mortem examination was ordered but Palmer managed to be present at it and spirited off the jar of stomach contents. Consequently, the results of the examination were inconclusive and a second examination was ordered. The toxicologist involved could find no evidence of poison but was convinced that poison had been used. An inquest was called and Palmer wrote to the coroner requesting that the verdict of death be given as 'natural causes'. He kindly enclosed a £10 note with his letter! Unfortunately for Palmer the verdict was 'deceased died of poison wilfully administered by William Palmer'.

It was believed that Palmer would not get a fair trial in Staffordshire and so he was sent for trial at the Old Bailey in London. During his trial, various pharmacists admitted to selling Palmer strychnine. His financial problems were laid out in detail and reference was made to the deaths of other people associated with him. He was found guilty and sentenced to death by hanging. In 1856, when his sentence was carried out, executions still took place in public and thirty thousand people turned up to see him die. As he stood on the gallows, Palmer is reputed to have looked at the trapdoor and asked if it was safe!

Another notable poisoner who used strychnine as his modus operandi was Dr Thomas Cream. He obtained his first medical degree in Canada and then took additional qualifications in London and Edinburgh. After being accused of murder and blackmail in Canada, Cream fled to Chicago. Here he set up a practice in the red-light district offering illegal abortions to prostitutes. A number of his patients died from strychnine poisoning but he himself was not implicated in their deaths. Then Cream made a major error. One of his patients died of strychnine poisoning after being supplied with a remedy for epilepsy. The death was put down to natural causes but Cream blamed the pharmacist who had filled the prescription and tried to blackmail him. Cream was arrested along with his mistress who had procured poison from Cream so that she could get rid of her husband. She turned state's evidence to avoid jail and Cream was sentenced to life imprisonment.

Cream was released from prison after serving ten years and came to London. He set up practice in Lambeth and again began offering services to prostitutes. Over the next six months, four prostitutes died from strychnine poisoning. The police were unable to identify the person responsible but the press called him the Lambeth Poisoner. After each death, Cream tried to implicate a prominent person and then offer to keep quiet in return for cash. One prostitute who was killed by Cream was Matilda Clover. Cream accused a fellow doctor,

William Broadbent, of poisoning Clover and demanded money in return for his silence. Broadbent sent the blackmail letter to the police who, until then, were unaware that Matilda Clover had been murdered. Clover was an alcoholic and her death was thought to have been brought about by her drinking. Murder had not been considered. Her body was exhumed and, on close examination, it became clear that she had been poisoned with strychnine.

Once it was confirmed that Clover had been murdered the police began to suspect that Cream was the infamous Lambeth Poisoner. They kept Cream under surveillance and made enquiries about him in the US. This revealed his previous conviction in Chicago for poisoning. Then, an event occurred which could have come straight out of a crime novel. Cream met a detective from New York who was visiting London and was fascinated by the story of the Lambeth Poisoner. Cream took the detective on a tour of the area and gave him details of where all the victims had lived and how they had died. The detective was very suspicious of Cream's detailed knowledge of the murders and alerted the British police. Cream was arrested and charged with the murder of four prostitutes, the attempted murder of a fifth and attempting to obtain money by extortion.

Cream was found guilty after a trial lasting four days and he was sentenced to death. One year after he came to England, Cream was hanged in Newgate Prison. The hangman claimed that Cream's last words were, "I am Jack the..." and tried to convince people that he had executed the notorious Jack the Ripper. However, Cream was in prison in Chicago when the Ripper murders took place in London... but it makes a good story!

Death in the arms of Morpheus

Opium is the dried latex obtained from unripe capsules of the opium poppy that has the scientific name *Papaver somniferum*. The specific epithet '*somniferum*' means 'sleep inducing' and describes one of the effects of opium consumption. In this regard, there are Egyptian hieroglyphics showing mothers giving their children opium capsules to lick like lollipops, presumably to keep them from crying. A 17th century English physician called Thomas Sydenham developed an alcoholic extract of opium latex that he called laudanum. This was recommended for the treatment of almost any ailment and was a staple of the medicine cupboard up until the early 20th century.

Opium latex contains a mixture of alkaloids and the two most significant ones are morphine and codeine. Both can be used for pain relief but morphine is far and away the most powerful. Morphine was first purified in the early 1800s and its name is derived from Morpheus, the Greek God of dreams who appears in Ovid's 'Metamorphoses'. The chemist who purified it tested it on himself and three friends: they experienced severe nausea and fell asleep for twenty-four hours. When administered in the correct dose it is very effective at relieving pain and use of this property was facilitated by the invention of the hypodermic syringe in the 1850s. However, soon it was realised that morphine is very addictive. Codeine chemically is very similar to morphine but has moderate pain-relieving properties and is much less addictive.

Morphine has proven to be an excellent drug for relieving the extreme pain of patients suffering from certain types of terminal cancer. However, the drug also is a very powerful respiratory depressant and this often causes death before the cancer does. This effect of morphine has not gone unnoticed and it has been the poison of choice for a number of mass murderers. One of these was Dorothea Waddingham who was hanged in 1936 for the poisoning of a number of patients in her unregistered nursing home. More recently, general practitioner Dr Harold Shipman became Britain's most prolific serial killer when he was convicted in 2000 for the murder of at least two hundred and forty patients. The exact number that he poisoned over a period of twenty-three years never will be known and suspicion about his activities only arose when he attempted to forge the will of his last victim. Shipman was sentenced to life imprisonment and hanged himself in prison. At the time of writing, a GP in Gosport, England is under investigation for the possible killing of six hundred and fifty (!) patients by poisoning them with morphine. So, the newest of poisons has been involved in more murders, at least in the West, than any of the old poisons. The fact that the perpetrators of the crimes are qualified doctors probably reflects the tight regulation today of poisons.

PLANT PORTRAIT: THE OPIUM POPPY

The genus *Papaver* consists of approximately seventy species of annual, biennial and perennial plants from a wide variety of habitats. They are indigenous to Europe and temperate Asia but a few originate from Australia, South Africa and the west coast of the US. About ten to twelve species are in cultivation and the best-known ones are:

Papaver nudicaule (Icelandic poppy)
Papaver rhoeas (the field poppy or Remembrance poppy)
Papaver cambricum (the Welsh poppy)
Papaver commutatum (the ladybird poppy)
Papaver orientale (Oriental poppy)
Papaver somniferum (the opium poppy)

The Oriental poppies are perennials and are the ones most seen in gardens. Many of them are hybrids with *P. bracteatum* or *P. pseudoorientale*. There are many named varieties and nine of them have been awarded the Award of Garden Merit by the Royal Horticultural Society. The oriental poppies do not produce morphine or codeine. The ladybird poppy is an annual that gets its common name because the petals are bright red with black spots. Like all the annual species, it seeds prolifically and is difficult to eliminate once you introduce it to your garden.

The opium poppy is very similar in appearance to the Oriental poppy but is an annual species. It is often grown in gardens for its large blue-green seed pods that are much favoured in dried flower arrangements. All varieties of the Oriental poppy produce morphine, codeine and other alkaloids but the ones used for the legal commercial production of these drugs are special high-yielding cultivars.

Colchicine: a rarely used poison

Medicinal preparations of the colchicine plant, *Colchicum autumnale*, were recommended for people with joint pain as early as 1500 BC. Benjamin Franklin is credited with introducing this therapy into the United States in 1763 for the treatment of gout. The active ingredient, colchicine, is still used today to treat episodes of acute gout and also is effective in treating familial Mediterranean fever. There are reports of colchicine being used to commit suicide but reports of deliberate poisoning are rare. The best-documented case was in the United States where a married man who had been in good health was admitted to hospital with nausea, vomiting, profuse diarrhoea and severe abdominal pain. After forty-eight hours in hospital, with his wife by his side, his condition deteriorated suddenly and he died. An autopsy failed to identify any significant abnormalities and the body was buried.

Several months later, a man who owned a chemical supply store contacted the police. The wife of the deceased had been in his store several months before her husband's death and purchased his entire stock of colchicine (thirty grams). She stated that she was using the substance to sanitise the water in the swimming pool (!) that she and her husband owned. She had paid for the colchicine with a cheque that later was returned by the bank because the account had been closed. An investigation was launched and included a re-analysis of a retained serum sample from the patient. The serum sample was found to contain a toxic level of colchicine and the deceased's wife went to prison.

The glory lily (*Gloriosa superba*) is a climbing plant that features an exotic red flower and which grows widely in tropical parts of Africa, Asia and Australia. It belongs to the same plant family as *Colchicum autumnale* and, like it, produces colchicine. A man in Sri Lanka was admitted to hospital with profuse vomiting and diarrhoea after drinking coriander tea, a local remedy for treating the common cold. Family members of the patient suspected poisoning by

Gloriosa because they had seeds at home and the victim's sister in law, who had made the tea, had fled the family home. Examination of the teapot revealed seeds of *Gloriosa* which resemble coriander seeds. The patient was lucky to survive but needed intensive care for nearly two weeks.

PLANT PORTRAIT: AUTUMN CROCUS

Colchicum autumnale, commonly known as autumn crocus, meadow saffron or naked ladies, is an autumn-blooming flowering plant that resembles the true crocuses, but is a member of the Colchicaceae plant family, unlike the true crocuses which belong to the family Iridaceae. The name 'naked ladies' comes from the fact that the flowers emerge from the ground long before the leaves appear. Despite the vernacular name of 'meadow saffron', this plant is not the source of saffron. *Crocus sativus* is the source of saffron and, confusingly, that plant also is referred to as the autumn crocus.

TRIAL BY ORDEAL AND THE DEATH OF 'ADAM'

Old Calabar or Duke Town, was an Efik city-state that flourished in the 19th century in what is now southern Nigeria. Scottish missionaries arrived there in 1846 to try and convert the Efik people to Christianity. It was not long before they became aware of native belief in the power of the seeds of a local plant to determine whether individuals were innocent or guilty of witchcraft or some serious misdemeanour. The seeds were those of a previously unknown legume and soon referred to as the Calabar bean, although the locals called them chopping nuts. The beans were crushed and soaked in water and the accused was made to drink the resulting milky extract. If the accused died, then they were guilty. If they lived, usually because they had vomited up the poison, then they were declared innocent. This became known to the missionaries as 'trial by ordeal' and they estimated that it was responsible for about one hundred and twenty deaths annually.

Over time, it became clear that trial by ordeal was a lot more sophisticated than simply giving people extracts of the bean. Innocent people often would volunteer to undergo the ordeal to show that only the guilty would suffer. The same was true in central Madagascar where the beans from a different plant, the Tangena tree (*Cerbera manghas*), were used. The person making the extracts could vary the toxicity and could even use different beans for people who were innocent.

Mary Slessor grew up in the slums of Dundee in Scotland. By the age of fourteen she was a skilled jute worker putting in a twelve-hour day. Her mother was a devout Presbyterian who was an avid reader of the Missionary Record and this led Mary to become a missionary. In 1876 she arrived in Calabar and discovered some horrific practices of which trial by ordeal was just one. Another was the belief that the birth of twins was an evil curse. Natives feared that the father of one of the infants was an evil spirit but, unable to determine which twin was fathered by the evil spirit, both babies were abandoned in the bush. Slessor learned to speak Efik and by living among the local people, gained their respect. In this way she was able to stop both the infanticide of twins and the use of trial by ordeal.

The parent church of the missionaries was in Edinburgh and so some of the Calabar beans found their way back there along with details of trial by ordeal. A toxicologist of some repute, Robert Christison, investigated the effects of the beans to the extent of eating part of one himself and documenting the consequences. That was in 1855. Six years later, John Hutton Balfour who was Regius Keeper of the Edinburgh Botanic Garden, produced a comprehensive account of the bean plant that he called *Physostigma venenosum*. The specific epithet *'venenosum'* means poisonous. In 1863, a young Edinburgh ophthalmologist, Argyll Robertson, published a paper documenting the use of an extract of Calabar bean to constrict the pupil of the eye. This extract was given the name physostigmine after the botanical name of the parent plant.

Robertson had a friend, Thomas Fraser, who was a doctor and who was the first to detail the effects of systematic administration of physostigmine. Like William Withering who pioneered proper clinical trials with digitalis (see p88), Fraser was rigorous in his experimental design. He used only one species of animal and ones of the same weight, he adjusted doses of the drug for bodyweight, he determined the minimum lethal dose and he undertook sufficient studies so that his results were statistically significant. Robertson had shown that physostigmine will constrict the pupils of the eye and others (p76) had shown that atropine will dilate the pupils. Therefore, Fraser reasoned, physostigmine could be used to counteract the effects of atropine poisoning. The converse also is true: atropine can be used to reverse the effects of compounds like physostigmine. This was put to good use in 1871 when forty-five children and one adult became ill after eating Calabar beans that had been dropped during the unloading of cargo at Liverpool docks. Prompt treatment with atropine saved all but one of them. Another early use of physostigmine was treating the spasms and seizures caused by tetanus. As one doctor wrote in 1874, "So many cases have been successfully treated within these few years by means of the Calabar bean, that I think it should be preferred in the treatment of this dangerous malady to any of these empirical remedies formerly recommended."

Almost sixty years after Fraser's work on physostigmine its chemical structure was elucidated and a detailed explanation was provided for its toxicity. Whilst new medical uses for it were found, it did not appear to be used to murder anyone except in Agatha Christie's novel 'Curtain'. That is, not until a ritual killing in London.

The torso in the Thames

In a quiet child's plot in a London churchyard, four Metropolitan Police detectives watched as a small, pastel blue coffin decorated with teddy bears was lowered into a grave. The coffin contained only the torso of an unidentified coloured boy to whom the police had given the name 'Adam'. The police officers were the only mourners. It was February 2007 and more than five years had passed since Adam's headless and limbless body had been found floating in the river Thames near the reconstructed version of Shakespeare's Globe theatre. It was a discovery that would start an investigation lasting over ten years and lead detectives into the dark world of human sacrifice, child trafficking and ritual homicide.

Forensic analysis of Adam's body suggested that he was five or six years old, he had been well-nourished and had not suffered abuse, sexual or otherwise. The body had been drained of blood and the head and limbs had been removed very skilfully. This suggested ritual killing as did the finding that Adam's first vertebra, the one between neck and spine, had been removed. This is known in parts of Africa as the Atlas bone for it is said to be the bone on which the mythical Atlas carried the world. In muti, traditional South African medicine, it is believed to be the centre of the body where all nerve and blood vessels meet and where all power is concentrated.

The composition of our bones reflects the mineral composition of the water that we drink and the food that we eat. A sophisticated analysis of the minerals in Adam's bones revealed levels of strontium, copper and lead much higher than would be found in a British child. Rather, it indicated that he had spent most of his short life living in Nigeria, somewhere around the city of Benin. Analysis of Adam's DNA confirmed that he was of Nigerian origin.

Analysis of the contents of Adam's gut was equally informative. Pollen was found in the large intestine and all of it was from plants such as alder that are native to Britain and north-western Europe. This indicated that he had spent some time in this region prior to his death. Plant extracts also were found and after a great deal of effort were identified as remnants of *Datura* leaves (see p78) and Calabar beans. Both plants are native to Nigeria and Calabar beans are only found there. This was further evidence of a Nigerian link to Adam. More worryingly, it suggested ritual killing because the Calabar bean was fed to human sacrifices to paralyse them while keeping them conscious. Adam could have been awake and conscious as the knife cut through his body. The final indicator of ritual killing was the presence of flecks of gold in the intestines: these would have been used to make the sacrifice more appealing to whatever god was being worshipped.

The only clothing that Adam had been wearing when he was found was a pair of bright orange shorts, size five to seven years. They carried the label Kids & Co, the brand name for Woolworths in Germany. Detectives established that they came from a batch of eight hundred and twenty pairs that had been sold in three hundred and twenty German and Austrian stores. The trail then went cold. The only other thing that detectives learned was that orange is a colour often linked to muti.

Following the discovery of Adam's body, detectives trawled through London's many ethnic communities. They heard many stories of muti ceremonies taking place, but there were no hints of a child killing or even a missing child. Painstaking checks of the attendance registers at over three thousand nurseries and schools found no evidence of a missing child who tallied with what was known about Adam. The picture that was building up was of a Nigerian child trafficked to Britain, possibly via Germany, for the purpose of being sacrificed. Worse still, according to Unicef, up to two hundred thousand children a year are trafficked out of West Africa every year to be sold for slave labour, sex work and possibly sacrifice.

A potential breakthrough came in 2003. Immigration officers at Glasgow airport arrested a confused Nigerian woman who had newly arrived from Germany. Her name was Joyce Osagiede. She was claiming asylum for herself and two young daughters and making claims about 'extreme religious ceremonies' in which her estranged and violent husband was engaged. The Metropolitan Police team investigating Adam's death immediately headed to Scotland. Searching the woman's belongings, they found a pair of orange shorts identical to the ones worn by Adam.

Investigators in Germany discovered that a young boy had been seen in Joyce's care, only to vanish shortly before Adam's body was found floating in the Thames. Meanwhile, both her estranged husband and another man she associated with had been convicted of offences relating to people trafficking. But Joyce denied ever having any contact with Adam and insisted she had only ever bought one pair of orange shorts. DNA tests showed she wasn't related to Adam in any way. Then, when it became clear that she had definitely been in Hamburg at the time of the boy's death, police had no choice but to release her. She was deported to Nigeria.

Ronke Phillips, a British journalist with Nigerian parents, had been following the case since Adam's body was first discovered. She was convinced that Joyce knew a lot more than she had told police. She kept in touch with the investigation team in London and with contacts in the Nigerian police. After a number of false starts, Joyce finally agreed to talk to Ronke in 2011. She said that when she lived in Germany she had looked after the boy as a favour to a friend who was about to be deported. The friend was not the boy's mother. Joyce then handed the boy over to a man that she called Bawa, who was going to take him to London. The boy's name was Ikpomwosa and he was killed in a 'ritual in the water'.

In 2013 Joyce Osagiede made further contact with Ronke Phillips. She wanted to tell the truth. The boy's name was really Patrick Erhabor and his mother was a friend of hers. The man she had given Patrick to was Kingsley Ojo who had been convicted ten years earlier of people trafficking and deported. Because of Joyce's mental state her evidence was not considered sound and Ojo had denied any involvement in Adam's death. The case is now closed and remains the only murder in the UK in which Calabar beans were involved.

PLANT PORTRAIT: Physostigma venenosum

The plant is a large, herbaceous, climbing perennial that can attain a height of fifty feet (fifteen metres). It belongs to the family Fabaceae and like all legumes, produces pods containing seeds. The pods are brown in colour and have a characteristic hook at one end which is reflected in the generic name '*Physostigma*'. Each pod contains two or three seeds (beans) that are about six to seven inches (fifteen to eighteen cm) long. The plant is native to tropical Africa and in temperate countries is not seen out of greenhouses in botanic gardens.

STATE-SPONSORED MURDER: POISONING POLITICAL OPPONENTS

Aficionados of the James Bond novels will know that Ian Fleming conjured up ever more fanciful ways for the enemies of agent 007 to kill him. The stories were entertaining but hardly believable and the recent film versions even less so. But, as we know, fact can be stranger than fiction. This is certainly true when we consider some of the assassinations carried out by the former Soviet Union and its successor, the current Russian state. What they have done could have come straight out of a Bond novel.

In 1921, soon after the Soviet Union was established, a poison laboratory was created under the name 'Special Office'. In true Soviet fashion, this was imaginatively re-labelled as Laboratory 1 in 1939 and was under the direct control of NKVD chief Lavrenty Beria. The head of the laboratory was Grigory Mairanovsky. He had been the head of several secret laboratories in the Bach Institute of Biochemistry in Moscow. In his new role he pioneered the use of political prisoners for experiments with poisons including digitoxin, ricin, curare and others. His PhD thesis was a good example of his activities: it was entitled 'Biological activity of the products of interaction of mustard gas with [human] skin tissues'. Mairanovsky also participated personally in a number of political assassinations including that of Swedish diplomat

Raoul Wallenberg who died in mysterious circumstances whilst in the custody of the KGB.

Following Stalin's death and the execution of Beira, Laboratory 1 was re-named Laboratory 12. In 1978 the laboratory became the Central Investigation Institute for Special Technology and was run by the First Chief Directorate of the KGB. Then, following the collapse of the Soviet Union, several laboratories were established for the 'creation of biological and toxin weapons for clandestine operations in the West', including Scientific Research Institute No2 outside Moscow. Throughout its history, the goal of the laboratory has been to find a tasteless, odourless poison that could not be detected post-mortem. Whilst that once might have been possible, modern analytical technology is such that anything can be detected — provided that you have an idea what might have been used!

There is a long list of victims of poisons developed by the Soviets including many of their own nationals. One high profile target was Alexander Solzhenitsyn who is best remembered for his books documenting Soviet abuses. In 1962 he received literary fame for 'One Day in the Life of Ivan Denisovich', which described the horrors of the forced labour camps better known as gulags. This was published with official approval during the political thaw under Stalin's successor, Nikita Khruschev. His next book, 'Cancer Ward', described his experience with cancer. This had developed whilst in a gulag in Kazakhstan but went into remission following treatment in a hospital in Tashkent. This was followed by 'The First Circle', a novel which depicts the lives of the occupants of a sharashka (experimental research station) located in the Moscow suburbs. Both books were published in the West but were only available as clandestine editions in the Soviet Union.

After Khruschev's removal in 1964, the cultural climate again became more repressive. Publishing of Solzhenitsyn's work quickly stopped and, as a writer, he became a 'non-person'. Solzhenitsyn received the ultimate accolade in 1970 when he was awarded the Nobel Prize for Literature. He accepted the award but refused to travel to Scandinavia to receive it for fear of not being allowed to return home. He now was sacrificing everything to write 'The Gulag Archipelago', his epic portrait of the labour camps, including collecting information from over two hundred former inmates. By now, Solzhenitsyn was becoming an embarrassment to the Soviet authorities and it was decided to eliminate him.

In 1971 Solzhenitsyn travelled to Novokerchassky in Rostovskaya Region to meet eyewitnesses to the recent shooting of unarmed workers who were protesting at low wages and the sudden rise in food prices. Later in the day, he began to feel unwell and returned to Moscow. He had severe stomach pains and his personal doctor, whom he trusted, diagnosed that he had been poisoned but not with something that he knowingly had consumed. For days he could hardly leave his bed or even lift his head but eventually he recovered. Strangely, the idea of an assassination attempt never occurred to him or his family. Years later, a retired KGB officer called Boris Ivanov admitted that Solzhenitsyn's mystery illness was the result of a botched attempt to poison him with ricin. It had been administered whilst he had been buying cookies in a store in Novokerchassky.

Ricin is a protein that is produced in the seeds of the castor oil plant, *Ricinus communis*. It is extremely toxic: a dose of purified ricin the size of a few grains of table salt can kill an adult human. It is toxic by inhalation, ingestion or injection. When it is ingested its effects are restricted to the gastro-intestinal tract where the initial symptoms are pain, inflammation and mucosal haemorrhage. These can be followed by severe nausea, vomiting and difficulty swallowing. These are the effects from which Solzhenitsyn suffered. If ricin is inhaled an allergy develops and the symptoms include watery eyes, swollen lips and difficulty in breathing. Injection of ricin results in major organ failure.

It is likely that the technique for using ricin was not fully developed when the attempt was made on Solzhenitsyn's life even though the KGB had fully expected it to work. We now know that the KGB learned from the botched assassination and they went on to develop a better way of administering the poison. In 1978 they got the chance to put this to the test, but outside of the Soviet Union. On August 26, Bulgarian émigré Victor Kostov and his wife were coming out of the Paris Metro when someone bumped into them. Kostov felt a pin-prick in his buttock but thought nothing of it, especially as the person had apologised to them.

Georgy Markov was another Bulgarian émigré, but one who was working for the BBC's Bulgarian service. On September 7, he was standing in a bus queue on Waterloo Bridge in London when a passer-by jabbed him with an umbrella. His assailant apologised in accented English before hailing a passing taxi and leaving the scene. That evening Markov felt unwell and noticed that there was a tiny pimple oozing blood on his right calf. The next day he mentioned the incident to his work colleagues which was fortunate because shortly afterwards he was admitted to hospital where he died on September 11. The information from Markov's colleagues focussed the attention of the police and the forensic pathologist on the wound from the umbrella. They recovered a tiny (two mm) platinum-iridium alloy capsule. When examined at the UK's Porton Down facility the capsule was found to contain traces of ricin.

The Markov incident prompted Kostov to return to hospital where an X-ray showed the presence of a tiny foreign body in his buttock, just where he had felt the pin-prick. This foreign body was removed by microsurgery and found to be identical to the one recovered from Markov. It too, contained ricin but for some reason the poison had not been released from the capsule. Had the capsule not been removed Kostov could have died at some time in the future when there would have been no link to the incident outside of the Paris Metro. The involvement of the Bulgarian secret police was strongly suspected and it was known that they would only have used ricin with the help of the KGB. The KGB denied all involvement but their role was confirmed by the high-profile defectors Oleg Kalugin and Oleg Gordievsky. In 2005 the assassin was identified as Francesco Giullino, a Dane of Italian origin who worked for the Bulgarian equivalent of the KGB. It is believed that in both the Kostov and Markov assassination attempts the poison had been administered by a gun disguised to look like a furled umbrella. James Bond would have approved!

Three years after the assassination of Markov, a former CIA agent called Boris Korczak was shot with a ricin pellet while shopping in Vienna, Virginia. He survived the attempt to kill him and claimed that the KGB was responsible because previously he had infiltrated their organisation. In 2001 the tables nearly were turned. The Information Telegraph Agency of Russia reported that officials had intercepted a conversation between two Chechen rebels discussing the use of a 'homemade poison' against Russian soldiers. The home of Chechen Brigadier-General Rizvan Chitigov was raided where a hoard of castor oil beans and instructions for purifying ricin were found.

The castor oil plant is easy to grow and it will thrive outside in warm climates such as the southern United States where it is grown commercially. Anyone with some basic biochemical knowledge can extract and purify the ricin contained in the beans. Given this, it is not surprising that there have been numerous attempts by civilians to poison politicians. In March 2003, US authorities intercepted two ricin-containing letters addressed to President George W Bush. The letters were sent by a person who said that they owned a trucking company and were angered over changes to federal trucking regulations. The FBI offered a $100,000 reward for information leading to an arrest but the money was never claimed.

In 2013, two anonymous letters sent to Michael Bloomberg, mayor of New York City, were found to contain traces of ricin. A similar letter was sent to the Washington DC offices of Mayors Against Illegal Guns and then one was sent to President Barack Obama. The perpetrator was a bit-part actress from Texas called Shannon Richardson. She tried to frame her husband for the crime but there were inconsistencies in her story and she failed a lie detector test. A jury found her to be guilty and currently she is serving a sentence of eighteen years in jail.

The most recent attempts to target politicians with ricin happened in October 2018. Letters laced with ricin were sent to Secretary of Defense James Mattis, Admiral John

Richardson who was Chief of Naval Operations and President Trump himself. At the time of writing, nobody had been arrested for the offences.

PLANT PORTRAIT: THE CASTOR OIL PLANT (Ricinus communis)

The plant is a member of the Euphorbiaceae, the spurge family. It is indigenous to the south-eastern Mediterranean basin, east Africa and India but is widely grown elsewhere as an ornamental plant. The false castor oil plant, *Fatsia japonica*, is similar in appearance but is completely unrelated. The generic name *Ricinus* is Latin for tick and is so named because the seeds have markings and a bump at the end that resemble ticks. The specific epithet *communis* means 'universal' and refers to its widespread distribution. The common name 'castor oil' probably comes from its use as a replacement for castoreum, a perfume base made from the dried perineal glands of the beaver (generic name *Castor*). After the flowers are fertilised, the plant develops spiny, greenish to reddish-purple fruits that contain shiny seeds that are known as castor oil beans.

The plant has been grown commercially for its oil which readers of a certain age will remember being used as a foul-tasting laxative when they were a child. Today, gentler and more pleasant laxatives are available. Castor oil is an effective lubricant and was used in World War I aeroplanes, some racing cars and model aeroplanes. Historically, it was used for lubricating two stroke engines due to its high heat resistance but it has been replaced with synthetic oils that are more stable and less toxic.

Poisoning with heartbreak grass

Sir Arthur Conan Doyle is best known for his stories about Sherlock Holmes but he started life as a physician. It was the diagnostic prowess of one of his lecturers at the University of Edinburgh Medical School that formed the basis of the deductive powers of his fictional detective. In the summer of 1879, when he was just twenty years old, Doyle was working in a general practice in what today is the Birmingham suburb of Aston. He had become curious after using tincture of gelsemium to treat neuralgia and noting that overstepping the advised dose appeared to have no ill-effects. Obviously prone to experimentation, Doyle was determined to ascertain how far one might go in taking the drug and what the primary symptoms of an overdose might be.

Doyle prepared a fresh tincture and dosed himself at the same time each day. At low doses of forty and sixty minims he observed no effects but after ingesting ninety minims he experienced extreme giddiness. After taking one hundred and twenty minims, the giddiness was lessened but several hours later he had vision problems. Psychological problems were gone after taking a dose of one hundred and fifty minims but he had headaches and diarrhoea. The maximum dose that Doyle took was two hundred minims and that caused unbearable diarrhoea, headache and a weak pulse. In a letter to the British Medical Journal, entitled 'Gelsemium as a poison', he concluded that healthy adults may take up to ninety minims but at higher doses the drug induces mild paralysis.

Doyle was very lucky in his self-experimentation with tincture of gelsemium. This tincture is an extract of the roots of a North American vine called *Gelsemium sempervirens* and contains a variety of alkaloids. The main alkaloid is a highly toxic compound called gelsemine which is much like strychnine. Despite this, there is only one documented case in the West of murder using the drug and that was in 1908. The situation in Asia is quite different.

Whereas *Gelsemium sempervirens* and *G. rankinii* are native to North America, *G. elegans* is native to most of Asia. It is an evergreen shrub which grows as a twining vine up to a height of twelve metres (thirty-eight feet). It may interweave with other edible plants or be mistaken for therapeutic herbs that have a similar appearance, leading to inadvertent consumption and poisoning. This is quite common. *G. elegans* is highly poisonous due to its strong neurological and respiratory depressive effects and can kill within thirty minutes if a lethal dose is ingested. In Hong Kong and other parts of China the plant is notorious for its use in murder and suicide and is known as 'heartbreak grass' or 'Gou-men' (lethal kiss).

In 2011, Chinese billionaire Long Liyuan was murdered whilst having lunch with local government official Huang Guang and two others. Long was about to expose the corruption of Huang. The latter slipped some gelsemium into the cat meat stew that they were eating and, in an attempt to cover up his crime, ate some of the food himself. All of the lunch party became sick and were hospitalised and Long subsequently died. Meanwhile, in Vietnam, a woman murdered her husband and inadvertently two of his friends. Her husband beat her when he was drunk so she started having an extra-marital affair. After the men died, she confessed to having poisoned her husband's herbal wine with an extract of *Gelsemium elegans*. The men died within one hour of drinking the wine.

Heartbreak grass would have remained unknown in the West were it not for the suspicious death of Alexander Perepilichny. He was a financier who left Moscow in 2009 to live in the UK. In 2010, he gave Swiss prosecutors documents detailing the involvement of senior Russian officials in the theft of $230 million from a hedge fund in Moscow. Sergei Magnitsky was a lawyer working for the hedge fund, Hermitage Capital, who had exposed corruption at senior levels. He was arrested in Moscow and died in prison after being beaten to death. After Magnitsky's death, Perepilichny obtained documents implicating tax officials and showing how they had laundered millions of dollars through Swiss bank accounts. Perepilichny was a marked man.

In November 2012, Perepilichny made a four-day trip to Paris where he booked two hotel rooms, one at a luxury hotel and the other at an ordinary three star hotel. He also spent more than £800 in a Prada designer fashion store but never took the items back to the UK. Nobody knew why he went to Paris or why he booked a five star hotel when he normally stayed in three star ones. Regardless, he returned from Paris on the Eurostar train. On arriving home, he felt unwell and decided to go for a jog to clear his head. Whilst out running he collapsed and died. At the subsequent inquest into his death it was reported that two autopsies had proved inconclusive and toxicology tests had found nothing unusual. The local police considered the case closed.

Perepilichny had taken out a large life insurance policy shortly before his death. As is normal, he had undergone medical tests before the policy was approved and, at forty-four years old appeared to be in good health. The life insurance company viewed Perepilichny's death as suspicious and ordered their own toxicology tests. Samples of stomach contents were sent for analysis to the Royal Botanic Gardens in Kew. Tests there found an unknown chemical compound that had the same molecular weight as five alkaloids from *Gelsemium elegans*, but its exact identity was unknown. Because of these findings, the inquest into Perepilichny's death was re-opened.

At the new inquest, a Ukrainian fashion designer said that she had met Perepilichny in Paris in 2012 not knowing that he was married and had children. They had spent two days at the five-star Hotel Bristol, and he had bought her a Prada handbag and Louis Vuitton shoes. However, he appeared stressed and did not pay much attention to her. On the night before he died, Perepilichny had eaten sushi and tempura but had sent the tempura back because it tasted bad. Later that night, when back in the hotel room, he had vomited three times in the bathroom. The next morning, he appeared to be fine and returned to London.

Had the Russian 'poison laboratory' finally found an undetectable poison and used it to murder Perepilichny? Taking the second question first, the answer has to be that we do not know because the UK government refused to release to the inquest many documents detailing the activities of Perepilichny. However, given the murder of Alexander Litvinenko with radioactive polonium and the 2018 attack on Sergei Skripal and his daughter in Salisbury with nerve agent, a Russian involvement in Pereplichny's death is highly probable. Have the Russians found an undetectable poison? Not if they use gelsemium alkaloids for a Chinese laboratory has developed a method for identifying these to facilitate diagnosis of cases of poisoning with *Gelsemium elegans*.

PLANT PORTRAIT: Gelsemium

There are three species of *Gelsemium*. Two of them are found in the south-eastern United States: the swamp jessamine (*G. rankinii*) and the yellow or Carolina jessamine or jasmine (*G. sempervirens*) which is the state flower of South Carolina. The third species, *G. elegans*, or 'heartbreak grass', is found throughout India, south-east Asia and China. *Gelsemium* is derived from 'gelsomino', the Italian word for jasmine, because they superficially resemble this plant. The specific epithet *sempervirens* means evergreen but all three species share this property.

The plants normally are found in woodland and because they grow as vines are usually to be found trailing through other shrubs. They are grown as ornamental plants because of their sweetly-scented, funnel-shaped flowers. Outside of sub-tropical areas they need to be grown in a cool or temperate greenhouse.

PEN PORTRAIT: WILLIAM SHAKESPEARE AND HIS PLANT POTIONS

Plant potions and poisons feature regularly in the works of Shakespeare (1564–1616) and the word 'poison' occurs eighty-four times. It is mentioned in twenty-seven plays, one sonnet and two poems. Readers will be familiar with the famous scene where Banquo and Macbeth come upon the three witches on the blasted heath. The witches are making a brew and one of the components is 'root of hemlock digged i' th' dark'. Not only is hemlock poisonous in its own right but Shakespeare emphasises this because in his time it was commonly believed that plants harvested in the dark acquired evil powers. Along with various animal components, such as eye of newt and toe of frog, the third witch adds '… and slips of yew sliver'd in the moon's eclipse'. Again, a reference to collecting material in the dark, in this case the berries of the yew tree which were well-known to be toxic.

Poison features multiple times in 'Hamlet'. The play starts when Hamlet's father is murdered by his uncle, Claudius. The ghost of Hamlet's father tells us what happened:

"Sleeping within my orchard
My custom always of the afternoon
Upon my secure hour thy uncle stole

With juice of cursed hebenon in a vial
And in the porches of my ears did pour
The leperous distilment, whose effect
Holds such an enmity with blood of man..."

The poison that Shakespeare calls 'hebenon' is most likely to be henbane. Although applying the otic route of administration seems odd to us, people in the 16th and 17th centuries believed that drugs could reach the rest of the body through the ear.

The mandrake, a source of scopolamine, features in no fewer than eight of Shakespeare's plays. The example that best illustrates the Bard's knowledge of it comes in 'Othello' when Iago says:

"Not poppy, nor mandragora
Nor all the drawing syrups of the world
Shall ever medicine thee to that sweet sleep
Which thou owedst yesterday"

In 'Romeo and Juliet', Friar Laurence prepares a potion for Juliet that when drunk will make her appear to be dead:

'And in this borrowed likeness of shrunk death
Thou shalt continue two and forty hours
And then awake as from a pleasant sleep'

Some writers have suggested that Juliet was given atropine but the effects of the drug are more like those of scopolamine. The fact that Juliet got her potion from a friar reflects the fact that during the Dark Ages, following the fall of the Roman Empire, knowledge of medicine was kept alive in the monasteries.

We are kept in the dark as to the poison that Romeo obtained from an apothecary as the only description given is:

"Put this in any liquid you will
And drink it off, and if you had the strength
Of twenty men, it would despatch you straight"

This poison could be almost any of the ones described in previous chapters. However, in other plays, Shakespeare clearly identifies the poison that he is using, e.g. aconite (Henry IV, part II) and hemlock (King Lear, Henry V).

The use of plants generally, and not just as poisons, reflect Shakespeare's vast medical knowledge for he used them in a way that apothecaries and doctors of the time would have used them. But from where did he get his knowledge? One source would have been his son-in-law, John Hall, who was a physician. Another source would have been the many herbals that were available. These were books containing a wealth of information about medicinal plants including ones by Dioscorides, Pliny the Elder, Galen and Avicenna. The one that probably influenced more than any other would have been John Gerard's 'Herball or Generall Historie of Plantes' that was published in 1597. Although much of this book was plagiarised from the works of others, it was the most widely-read botany book in English in the 17th century. Given that Gerard was based in Holborn and Shakespeare spent much of his time in London, it is more than likely that the two of them knew one another as London was a small place at the time.

PART FOUR:
THE POWER OF PLANTS IN SOLVING CRIMES

FORENSIC BOTANY IN THE INVESTIGATION OF SUSPICIOUS DEATHS

Forensic science is the application of scientific principles and techniques to matters of criminal justice, especially the collection, examination and analysis of physical evidence. Forensic botany is a sub-discipline of forensic science that involves the analysis of plants and plant parts and, as will be seen later, it has many applications in non-criminal settings. (Part Five, p187) It is not a new discipline, for it has its origins in a science known as pharmacognosy that developed in the 19th century. At that time, nearly all drugs were derived from plants and many of these were sourced from other continents. Adulteration and substitution of the imported plant materials was a major problem and biological analysis was developed as a routine quality control tool. By looking at the structure of the plant material, if it was intact, and its microscopic structure if it was either intact or pulverised, a trained pharmacognosist could establish if it was the material it claimed to be.

Forensic botany can be sub-divided into a number of specialties including plant anatomy and wood anatomy (the study of cellular features), plant systematics (species identification), palynology (the study of pollen), plant ecology (plant succession patterns) and limnology (freshwater ecology). While most of these involve microscopic analysis of samples, there is an additional tool that is finding particular use in non-homicide cases and that is profiling of plant DNA. Unless crime scene officers have an understanding of what forensic botany is, and how it can be used, there is a real danger that they will overlook or destroy vital evidence. In the examples below the police were perspicacious enough to make full use of plant-based evidence.

The Soham Murders

Until 2002 most people in Britain had never heard of Soham, a quiet town of about ten thousand inhabitants north-east of Cambridge. In August that year two ten-years-old girls, Holly Wells and Jessica Chapman, went missing. They had attended a barbecue at Holly's house on Sunday August 4, and at about 6.15 p.m. had gone out to buy some sweets. They were not seen alive again. At the time of their disappearance, they had been wearing replica Manchester United football shirts.

Ian Huntley was the caretaker at the local secondary school and his girlfriend, Maxine Carr, was a teaching assistant at the primary school attended by the missing girls. Following the girls' disappearance, Huntley appeared in several television interviews speaking of the shock in the local community. One news reporter even commented that Huntley might have been the last person to see the girls before they disappeared, something that Huntley agreed was possible. Huntley and Carr were questioned by police for over seven hours on August 16, twelve days after the girls went missing. Huntley's house and the school grounds were searched and at the latter site, the burned remains of the girls' clothing were found in a garbage bin.

Forensic analysis of the bin contents revealed some hairs from Huntley as well as his fingerprints and fibres from his carpet and curtains. Fibres matching the girls' shirts were found on Huntley and around his house, thereby establishing a two-way link between Huntley and the girls. This clearly indicated that the girls had been in Huntley's house but not necessarily on the night that they disappeared, even though they would have passed it when they went to buy sweets.

On the afternoon of August 17, the day after the search of Huntley's house, a local gamekeeper found two bodies in a ditch about twelve miles from Soham. The gamekeeper had noticed an 'unusual and unpleasant smell' in the area several days earlier and on smelling it again decided to investigate. The police called in forensic botanist Patricia Wiltshire and asked her to examine the site. Although the foliage around the site where the girls had been found appeared untouched, Wiltshire noticed an area where stinging nettles had sprouted new side shoots. These side shoots only grow when nettles have been damaged, for example, if someone has trampled on them. She was able to identify this as the point where the bodies had been taken into the ditch. Not only that, knowing the rate of growth of the shoots she was able to establish that the bodies had been dumped thirteen to fourteen days earlier. Had the police not called in Wiltshire when they did this, vital evidence would have been lost. A post-mortem examination of the bodies revealed that the girls had not died at the site where they were found: rather, they had been moved after they were murdered.

When questioned about the bodies, Huntley denied ever having been in the location where they were found. However, Wiltshire had analysed the soil from Huntley's car and items belonging to him. By comparing them to samples taken from the ditch she was able to prove that he had been there. Sixty-four different types of pollen, some from rare plants, were found in soil around the ditch and many also were found on Huntley's shoes, the pedals and footwell of his car and on a petrol can. A forensic examination of the car found traces of chalk, brick dust and concrete that matched the surface of the track where the bodies were found. All this evidence was recovered despite Huntly having washed the car thoroughly, replaced the floor mats and vacuumed it, and had the tyres replaced. The following year, at the Old Bailey in London, Huntley was convicted on two counts of murder and sentenced to a minimum term of forty years in prison.

Getting to the roots of time of death

In the case of the Soham murders, the time since the deposition of the bodies in the ditch was established from the pattern of nettle re-growth. The patterns of plant growth have been used in other cases to establish a time of death. In one case, a skeleton was found in a shallow grave and the brain cavity of the skull was filled with roots of a buttercup. The anatomy and developmental stage of the roots indicated that the plant was approximately one year old and this was supported by knowledge of the rate of buttercup growth. This suggested that the skeletal remains had been in this particular location for at least one year. The plant could have developed secondarily some time after the body was deposited so a maximum time estimate was not possible.

Root growth was used to establish time of death in another case, this time in Denver, Colorado. Cher Elder was reported missing in March 1993 but a few days later was seen on a casino video in the company of Thomas Luther, a man with a record of brutal sexual assaults. The police kept Luther under surveillance but made no progress. Then the police were told by an informant that Luther had bragged about killing a girl and burying her off Interstate 70 where the police would not find her. There was little the police could do until 1995 when a former cellmate of Luther's told police that he had been to the gravesite with Luther. He took the police to the area but no body was found. Six weeks later, Cher's former boyfriend was arrested in connection with a different homicide. He told police that he too had been to the gravesite and knew exactly where it was. He showed police the location and a body was recovered when a trench was dug. Dental records confirmed that the body was that of Cher Elder.

When Luther was arrested for the death of Cher Elder he claimed he was innocent and said that anyone could have killed her and buried her anytime since her disappearance. A forensic botanist was asked to examine the roots that had penetrated the gravesite. A detailed examination of the morphology of the roots indicated that they were approximately two years old. This fixed the time that the grave was dug, a time when Luther was not in prison. This was only circumstantial evidence of Luther's guilt but other evidence resulted in him being convicted for the murder.

In a different turn of events, unusual plant growth led to the discovery of a body. Between 1955 and 1964, the Mediterranean island of Cyprus was riven with violence between the Greek Cypriot and Turkish Cypriot communities. This was caused by Britain offering to cede control of the island and both Greece and Turkey laying claim to it. In 1962,

Ahmet Hergune and two compatriots were part of a resistance group who were spotted hiding in a cave by their Greek opponents. Dynamite was thrown into the cave and the resulting explosion likely killed all three. When Hergune failed to return from his mission, his family guessed that he had been killed but had no idea where his body was.

Forty-four years after Hergune went missing, a botanist on the island spotted a fig tree growing in an unusual place and decided to investigate. When he dug down to the tree's roots he uncovered the remains of a body that subsequently was identified as the man missing for all these years. How could this be? It turned out that the tree was growing out of the body cavity where the stomach would be and it is believed that it had developed from a fig seed in the gut contents. Normally a fig tree would not grow in a cave but the original explosion had blown a hole in the cave roof allowing light to flood in.

Linking the murderer to the scene of the crime

One day in 2010 a man in Fort Lauderdale, Florida, spotted a container floating in the canal outside his house. When he recovered the container he was shocked to find that inside it were arms and legs covered in concrete. One week later, in a different county, another man found a bucket containing a human head covered in concrete. Finally, two weeks later in yet another county, some fishermen found a human torso in a container floating in a different canal. Based on DNA analysis and fingerprinting, the body parts were confirmed as all belonging to the same man who was identified as Warren Danzig. Further investigation revealed that Danzig's address was the home of a man called Jamie Saffran.

When the police questioned Saffran they were told that he and Danzig were friends but the latter lived in the Dominican Republic and only used Saffran's home to get mail. Indeed, a plane ticket for a return flight to the Dominican Republic had been found with some of the body parts. Further investigation revealed that the ticket had been cancelled by telephone and that the call had been made by a cell phone found in Saffran's house. Next it was discovered that Danzig's credit card had been used to purchase tyres for a pickup truck after the body parts had been discovered and employees at the tyre store remembered Saffran. However, this did not necessarily mean that Saffran had killed Danzig but only that he had misused Danzig's credit card.

When the body parts were first discovered various plant remnants were mixed in with them. The police called in a botanist who was an expert in plant identification. He recognised that the plant parts came from two different cultivated plants: the umbrella tree (*Schefflera actinophylla*) and the Chinese privet (*Ligustrum sinense*). Although the umbrella tree was common in southern Florida, the botanist had never seen a specimen of Chinese privet growing there. However, on being taken to Saffran's house he found both plants growing side by side. This immediately put the house in the frame as the scene of the murder. A police search uncovered some blue rope identical to that found in the same container as the head, a shovel covered with concrete, a sledgehammer that tested positive for human blood and some sharp cutting tools.

In the Warren Danzig murder, for which Jamie Saffran subsequently was convicted, the identification of an uncommon plant (Chinese privet) ultimately led to the scene of the murder. In a different case, this time in Arizona, DNA evidence was used to link the murderer to the scene of the crime. The body of a woman called Denise Johnson was found in the countryside near some paloverde trees. Her clothing was scattered about the area and she had been bound with cloth and braided wire. During a close examination of the site, a phone pager was found and this belonged to a man called Mark Bogan. Bogan admitted that he had picked up Johnson, who had been hitchhiking, and that they had had sexual relations in his pickup truck. However, he and Johnson then had an argument and she stormed off taking his pager with her. He denied ever having been to the site where the body was found.

When Bogan's truck was examined the police found a number of seed pods which were identified as coming from a paloverde tree. A specialist in DNA analysis was called in and asked if he could determine if the seed pods had come from any of the trees where the body was found. Fortuitously, paloverde trees are outbreeding and all the wild trees were found to have a different DNA profile, as did ones from places frequented by Bogan. When the seed pods were tested their DNA profile matched one of the paloverde trees, the one where Johnson's body was found. Bogan subsequently received a life sentence for first degree murder.

It is not just macroscopic plants, i.e. ones that can be seen with the naked eye, which can be used to link a suspect to a crime scene: microscopic plants also can be used, a technique known as forensic limnology. One day in suburban Connecticut, two young boys were fishing at a pond when they were attacked by multiple teenaged assailants. The boys were accosted at knifepoint, bound with duct tape, beaten with a baseball bat and thrown into the pond to drown. One of the victims managed to free himself, rescue his friend and summon help from local residents. Three suspects were soon arrested but denied having been at the scene of the crime.

When the suspects were arrested their sneakers (trainers) were found to have mud and sediment on them. Analysis of the sediment revealed the presence of various freshwater algae including diatoms and scaled chrysophytes. The same micro-algae were found in the pond sediment suggesting, but not proving, that the suspects had been at the pond. Further analyses revealed that a particular chrysophyte was dominant in all samples and there was no significant difference in the ratios of three species of diatom. This confirmed that the suspects had lied about not being near the pond.

In another case of forensic limnology, a husband told police that he had come home and found his wife lying dead on the sofa. She had been struck on the head with a blunt object. Examination of the victim revealed abrasions to the body and plant material on her clothes. This plant material matched vegetation on the driveway and this led to the discovery of a brick in the pond behind the house. This brick was contaminated with hair and tissue of the victim. Had the husband killed his wife? The husband had been wearing a T-shirt when he said that he found the body. This T-shirt was stained and examination of the stains showed that they consisted of algae that matched those in the pond. This clearly established a link between the weapon (brick) and the assailant (husband).

Suicide or murder?

When a human body is found with significant injuries, one the first things that police try to determine is if the person committed suicide or if they were murdered. Often this can be surprisingly difficult but sometimes botanists can help as illustrated by two cases from Taiwan. In the first case, the body of a young woman was found lying in the gutter of a road. Because there was no obvious damage to the body it was thought at first that she had been the victim of a hit and run accident. During an initial examination of the body some plant material was found in her hair. This material consisted of a tiny berry and a plant stem. A botanical expert suggested that they came from a member of the Solanaceae, the potato family, but these were not native to the area. A more detailed search of the area where the body was found, uncovered another piece of stem from a similar plant. On looking upwards, the investigators saw some potted plants on a balcony some twelve feet above ground. The potted plants had identical foliage and berries to the material found in the victim's hair and were conclusively identified as being *Solanum nigrum*.

The above information led the police to think that the victim had fallen from the top of the building and that she made contact with the potted plants as she fell. In the process, some of the plant material was transferred to her hair and some fell in the gutter. A post-mortem examination found injuries consistent with the woman falling from a height. Subsequently, the woman's relatives told police that she had been depressed and had attempted suicide before.

In the second case, the body of a man was found hanging from a tree. Asphyxiation clearly was the cause of death but had he hung himself or had he been murdered? Investigators noted that he had moss smeared on the insides of his wrists and that identical moss was growing on the branch of the tree from where he had been suspended. The pattern of disturbance of the moss suggested that the moss had been transferred to the man's skin when he was tying the rope to the tree and the cause of death was given as suicide.

Concluding remarks

As every good detective knows, the crime perpetrator always leaves some trace of themselves at the scene and the scene always leaves some evidence on the perpetrator. If there are plants growing at the scene of the crime, then there will be plant evidence and investigators need to look for it. As the example of the Soham murders shows, no matter how hard you try to eliminate this evidence some incriminating traces will remain.

THE POWER OF POLLEN

On a clear day in September 1991, a German couple was hiking at an elevation of 10,500 feet in the Ötzal Alps on the Austrian-Italian border when they came upon a corpse melting out of the ice. The couple told the authorities who assumed that the body was that of a climber who had been lost on one of the glaciers that occur in this region. After the body was extracted, it was sent to nearby Innsbruck for examination and identification where a surprise was in store; the male victim was several thousand years old. He was given the name Ötzi, after the region where he was found, but where had he come from and what was he doing when he died? Answering these and other questions involved experts in different disciplines for the next twenty-five years.

The intense cold at the altitude where Ötzi's body was found meant that the gut contents had been preserved and analysis of these provided a wealth of information. Over thirty different types of pollen were found including those from wheat and legumes. Other pollen indicated that a meal had been eaten in a mid-altitude conifer forest shortly before death. Another type of pollen was particularly interesting. It was from the hop hornbeam (*Ostrya carpinofolia*) and the cell content within the pollen's outer shell was intact. This indicated that the pollen was fresh when Ötzi died because the inner cellular material of pollen from hop hornbeam dies within a few days of being shed. Since the pollen is produced in the late spring this must have been when death occurred. Also, Ötzi most likely came from a village on the Italian side of the Alps since the hop hornbeam grows there, but not on the Austrian side.

The story of Ötzi illustrates a number of important features of pollen. First, it is produced in such large amounts that it even makes its way into the intestinal tract. It certainly will get trapped in clothing and the nasal cavity and can be used to follow a person's movements. Second, it is highly resistant to destruction and decay and can remain intact for a long time, thousands of years in the case of Ötzi. If crime scene evidence is handled correctly, then years later pollen can still be recovered and used as evidence. Third, there are nearly five hundred thousand plant species that produce pollen and the pollen from each species has a distinctive architecture. In some cases, the pollen from closely related species is very similar but an expert, known as a palynologist, usually can identify the source down to the level of the plant genus. There is another feature of pollen that is important in criminal investigations: it is microscopic in size and individual grains are invisible to the naked eye. This means that it still can be found no matter how much cleaning a criminal does to cover up his misdeeds.

The first use of pollen analysis in a criminal investigation occurred in 1959 in Austria. A man disappeared whilst on a trip down the River Danube and his body could not be found. A friend and business partner of the missing man came under suspicion but the police had no evidence that he had been involved in the disappearance. During a search of the suspect's cabin police found a pair of muddy boots. These were given to a palynologist at the University of Vienna. He identified pollen from spruce, willow and alder trees as well as from a much rarer tree, hickory. Only a tiny piece of land in Austria had this unique mix of trees. When the suspect was confronted with this information he confessed that he had murdered his colleague and led the police to his grave.

Another case involving long-term survival of pollen occurred in Magdenburg, Germany in 1994. A mass grave was found that contained thirty-two male skeletons, but who had killed the men? One possibility was that they were victims of the Gestapo at the end of World War II in the spring of 1945. Another was that they were Soviet soldiers killed by the secret police after an East German revolt in the summer of 1953. A palynologist was invited to try and solve the mystery. He rinsed out the nasal cavities with saline to recover any pollen that was present and then set about identifying what he had found. Several of the skulls had high levels of pollen from plantain, rye and lime trees but none of these plants were pollinating at the time of the investigation. Since these three plants produce pollen in late summer, the victims most likely had been killed by the East German secret police.

Three years after the Magdenburg mass grave was found, pollen experts were working as part of the North East Bosnian Mortuary Team that was conducting investigations into Balkans war crimes. In Srebrenica, about seven thousand men were taken away, executed and buried in mass graves. Three months later the killers realised the mass graves were evidence of a massacre and so reburied the victims in smaller graves a long distance away. In this way, the killers could argue that the dead were victims of small skirmishes in the woods and not an act of mass genocide. Working under a constant UN guard, scientists, including Tony Brown from Exeter University, sampled pollen from the primary mass graves and the smaller, secondary graves. Analysis of the pollen on the victims, particularly in their nasal cavities, showed that much of it was from cereals. The original mass grave was in a wheat field but the secondary graves were in forests where there were no nearby cereal crops.

Pioneering forensic palynology

Following the pioneering use of forensic palynology in Austria described above, there were a number of other criminal cases in Europe where the technique also was used but these were few and far between. Rather, it was New Zealand on the other side of the world and with a population of just 4.5 million people where the police started making routine use of palynology evidence. It began in 1983 when a fourteen-year-old girl called Kirsa Jensen went missing whilst out riding her horse near Napier on North Island. Her horse later was found tethered to an old, World War II gun emplacement with a rope that was not hers. The police gave the rope to palynologist Dallas Mildenhall for examination. At that time, he had only ever examined fossilised pollen to date oil deposits.

Mildenhall extracted the rope with chemicals to release any trapped pollen and identified grains that came from broad beans, pumpkins and beetroot. This suggested that the rope had been owned by someone who grew vegetables. The police had a suspect who was a market gardener. When they searched his property they found an identical piece of rope with the same pollen content. When the case came to court it was decided that there was not enough evidence to convict the suspect and he was set free. The suspect committed suicide nine years later and, if he did kill Kirsa Jensen, he took the secret of her body's whereabouts to the grave.

Despite the lack of conviction in the Kirsa Jensen case, the police started using the services of Dallas Mildenhall on an almost routine basis. The task of the forensic palynologist is greatly simplified if they find pollen from rare plants that only grow in a restricted area. Mildenhall has helped solve at least two crime investigations after finding pollen from the silver birch tree that has very limited distribution in New Zealand. In one case a cowpat on the road at the site of a hit and run fatality was found to have a high content of silver birch pollen. A suspect was identified and cow dung on the tyre of their car had the same high percentage of silver birch pollen. In another case, a suspect denied being anywhere near the scene of a crime. A murder victim was found in a mountainous area where there were many silver birch trees. The suspect's jacket and shorts were contaminated with silver birch pollen despite his protestations that they had never left the city of Wellington where the tree does not grow.

It is not just the presence of rare pollen that is useful, the form it is in can also be very helpful, as another case shows. A young woman was pulled into an alleyway in Christchurch and violently raped. Although shaken, she was able to describe the assailant to the police and shortly after a man matching the description was arrested. The suspect admitted having been in the area and admitted to talking to her. He said that when he had seen her she seemed to be distressed but when asked she said that she was OK. Now, he claimed, she must be putting his face on the face of the rapist, because he had never been in the alleyway. There was no DNA evidence, but the police noted dirt-stains on his clothes. These, he said, came from his yard where he was working on his car.

The alleyway where the crime occurred was lined along one side by a row of low flowering shrubs of wormwood, *Artemisia arborescens*, which is native to the Mediterranean area. The shrubs had been broken and flattened during the struggle that led up to the rape. The suspect's clothes with the dirt stains were sent for pollen analysis together with a comparative sample of soil from the crime scene.

The soil sample was dominated, as might be expected, by pollen of *Artemisia*. Much of this pollen was in clumps, indicating that the source of it was the crime scene and that it had not merely blown in. The pollen of this genus has a very distinctive appearance making it easy to identify. The soil had a mix of fresh *Artemisia* pollen and somewhat older, darker coloured grains as well as an unusually large, thick-walled fungal spore. The same *Artemisia* pollen dominated the clothing sample, again occurring mainly in clumps, in a mix of fresh and older grains, and the same thick-walled fungal spore type was abundant. The percentage of *Artemisia* pollen was so high that the only explanation was that the clothing was in direct, forceful contact with a wormwood plant.

Investigators searched for wormwood near the suspect's home, and other places that he visited but found none. *Artemisia* species are not common in New Zealand, only being planted occasionally in gardens. The forensic laboratory had processed over one thousand pollen samples from many localities in New Zealand and never found *Artemisia* in more than a trace amount, so the chances of finding large amounts statistically were very low. The fungal spores were also very rare and so the chances of the suspect being contaminated with them and *Artemisia* pollen if he was not at the rape scene were vanishingly small. This pollen and spore evidence was presented at his trial where he was found guilty and given an eight-year prison sentence.

A totally different case involved the theft of three hundred sheep from a ranch on the South Island of New Zealand. A few weeks later, the rustler tried to sell them at a livestock auction on the North Island. Although the sheep had no markings on them, the auctioneer was suspicious. He knew the seller and that he was selling far more sheep that his small ranch could support. The police impounded the sheep and contacted the original owner who thought that they were his but could not prove this definitively. A small patch of wool was taken from the backs of several of the impounded sheep and sent for pollen analysis. The pollen types found matched those found in the original owner's pasture land and not those from the seller's land. The sheep were returned to their original owner and the rustler was convicted of theft.

A freak of nature helps catch a killer

A kayaker paddling along the Avon River near Christchurch, New Zealand spotted something entangled in the branches along the riverbank. Closer inspection showed it to be the body of a young woman. She was a prostitute called Mellory Manning and she had been working her usual pitch the previous evening. A post-mortem examination showed that she had been strangled, beaten with a metal pole and stabbed three times before being dumped in the river. The fact that the exit wounds on her back were small and similar meant that the knife that was used to kill her probably hit against a hard surface, i.e. she was lying on her back when she was killed. The pathologist also thought that Mellory's left arm had been positioned up in front of her head when she was murdered, again suggesting that she had been lying on her back.

In the previous twenty-four months, two other prostitutes had been murdered in Christchurch. Although the police did not think that they were linked there were whispers about the existence of a serial killer. So, the police were determined to find the person who murdered Mellory Manning. After interviewing hundreds of people, suspicion fell on members of a local gang called the Aotearoa Mongrel Mob who rented a warehouse and a vacant lot close to where Mellory's body had been found. The gang was involved in drugs and prostitution and one thought was that Mellory had crossed them. However, the police had no evidence to link them to the killing. Indeed, the police did not even know where the murder had taken place.

The police brought in Dallas Mildenhall to see if pollen analysis would help identify the murder location. The first sample was taken from the nose. If a victim is face down on the ground just before death there will be thousands of pollen grains in the nasal cavity. In the case of the samples from Mellory there was a relative dearth of pollen confirming the pathologist's view that she had been lying on her back when she was killed. But where had she been killed? The police brought Mildenhall dozens of samples from all over Christchurch but the pollen in them did not match that found on the body of Mellory. However, one sample was received that might be a match and it came from the address where the Mongrel Mob hung out.

Most of the vegetation growing in the vacant lot around

the Mongrel Mob's base was a grass known as ripgut brome. This was so common in the area around Christchurch that Mildenhall thought that it would be of little diagnostic value. That was until he noticed something very unusual. All pollen grains, regardless of the plant that they come from, have two things in common: a hard, outer shell and a single pore through which the genetic material exits. When examined with a microscope, some of the ripgut pollen from Mellory's clothing had two pores rather than one. In all the years of looking at pollen, Mildenhall had never seen grains with two pores.

Mildenhall theorised that the aberrant pollen grains were the result of a mutation caused by the plants being sprayed with a herbicide. When it was discovered that the vacant land next to the Mongrel Mob's headquarters had been sprayed with a herbicide one month before Mellory's murder the police began to get excited. Mildenhall was dubious about the value of this observation because if only one or two plants had been mutated then finding them would be like looking for the proverbial needle in a haystack. Nevertheless, after much searching of pollen samples from the land around the gang's property Mildenhall struck gold: he found some two-pored bromegrass pollen grains. He went back and looked at the pollen grains in all the other samples that the police had given him and none had two pores. The murder location had been found.

Armed with information about the scene of the murder, and other evidence, the police began to question individual members of the Mongrel Mob. Eventually one of them revealed details about the murder that he could only have known if he had been there. He stood trial, was found guilty and sentenced to life imprisonment — and a microscopic freak of nature, two-pored pollen, was pivotal in his indictment.

Forensic palynology outside New Zealand

In the previous chapter we saw how forensic botanist Patricia Wiltshire helped trap the killer of two girls in Soham near Cambridge, including using pollen to link the killer to the place where the bodies were found. This was just one of over two hundred cases in which she has been involved. It all started in 1995 when she received a phone call from Hertfordshire police. There had been a murder and the police wanted to know whether Wiltshire could say if a vehicle had been in a certain field. The partly burnt body of a man had been discovered there, and while the police suspected a gang of the killing, they had no evidence. But the field had been full of maize and, with laudable initiative, the senior investigating officer realised that there might be pollen from it on the gang's car.

Wiltshire was sent a soil sample from the car to analyse. Unfortunately, it was the wrong season for flowers and by now any maize pollen from the previous year had gone. But the soil sample did contain pollen from the arable weeds that grew around the edge of the field. It was enough for Wiltshire to conclude that the car had been parked close by, and that the killers had walked through the weeds on their way in and out of the field. She went to the crime scene and said to the police, "Don't show me where the body was, I'll show you." And she did: she picked out the exact spot where the body had been. Her evidence was so strong that when it was presented to the suspects they confessed to the murder. From that point on word spread and Wiltshire found her services being required in more and more investigations by police forces across Britain.

Witshire is particularly proud of her role in helping to solve a murder that had occurred nearly thirty years before. Christopher Laverack was nine years old in 1984 when he disappeared after leaving his mother's house in Hull to go and see his sister. Two days later his body was found wrapped in a carpet in a nearby stream. He had been sexually assaulted and beaten to death. Police the world over find the murder of children particularly reprehensible and the local police were particularly frustrated when they could find no leads to the killer. They suspected that Christopher's uncle, Melvyn Read, was involved despite him being described as 'lovable' by relatives but they had no hard evidence.

The first breakthrough in the case came in 2002 when several boys accused him of sexual abuse. He was convicted and went to prison in 2003. His sexual deviation made him a prime suspect for Christopher's murder and police re-opened the case. The clothing that Christopher was wearing when he was killed was sent to Wiltshire and she found unusual pollen and other plant matter that gave a direct link to Read's garden. She said that the link was so strong that it, "stood out like a beacon." A brick found with the body could also be linked forensically to the garden. By now Read had died so the police could not test their evidence in court. So, in 2012 they sought independent assessment of the strength of their case against Read to see whether there would have been a realistic chance of a conviction in court. The QC who did the assessment described the weight of evidence against Read as conclusive and the police finally closed the case. Nevertheless, as the detective leading the investigation said, "Only two people really know what happened that night, and both are dead."

The United States is one of the most technologically savvy countries in the world so it might come as a surprise to learn that forensic palynology is hardly ever used in the investigation of American homicides. There have been only a few notable cases. In one of these, police in New York State re-opened an investigation into a murder that had occurred twenty-seven years earlier. A teenage girl was shot in the forehead on a country road, dragged into a field and shot again in the back. She had never been identified and nobody had been apprehended for her killing. When her clothing was given to a forensic palynologist, he found in a pocket three (!) pollen grains from an Australian pine tree. If she had never left the US then these must have come from Florida or Southern California. If the victim was from either of these areas, it would explain why she had not turned up on the local databases of missing persons. Soon her details matched a missing girl from Florida and detectives finally had a name for her.

In June 2015, a pet dog was attracted to a rubbish bag on the shore of Deer Island, Boston. Inside the bag were the remains of a young female child but there were no clues to her identity. There had been some decomposition such that even her fingerprints were unreadable. She was given the name 'Baby Doe'. The National Center for Missing and Exploited Children suggested to the police that they get pollen analysis done and the task was assigned to Andrew Laurence at US Customs and Border Protection. Hair and clothing from Baby Doe contained a mix of pollen from oak and pine trees and other plants native to Massachusetts, indicating that she had lived locally. Of much greater interest was the presence of pollen from a particular species of cedar tree for the only specimen of this tree was in the Arnold Arboretum in a suburb of Boston. The police made detailed enquiries locally to the arboretum and soon they got reports of a child who had not been seen for some time. Her name was Bella Bond and her mother and the mother's boyfriend were charged with murder.

Tracking narcotics with pollen

Whereas the US makes little use of forensic palynology in homicide cases it makes full use of it in the war against drug trafficking. It started in November 2011 when eight thousand pounds of marijuana were seized in a warehouse in San Diego. Two weeks later, a similar amount of marijuana was seized one thousand miles away in Texas. Initially it was assumed that the two lots of marijuana had come from different Mexican cartels but pollen analysis suggested otherwise. Over the next six months there were lots of seizures of bulk marijuana across southern California, Arizona and Texas. All of them had an identical pollen print. More interesting was that this print included pollen from sagebrush. Although there are many varieties of sagebrush in the US there is only one variety in Mexico and it grows in a very specific location. This information was shared with the Mexican government and led to a raid on the production centre which was a farm outside Chihuahua.

With that first success in tracking marijuana, the US Customs and Border Protection (CBP) decided that pollen analysis could be useful in tracking other drug seizures. They needed a full-time palynologist and that was Andrew Laurence, who worked on the Baby Doe case described above. One of the early cases that he worked on was a cocaine seizure in Detroit. The cocaine was destined for Canada and was being carried on a truck whose manifest said that it had come from Salinas in California. The pollen trapped in the truck's air filter showed that it had travelled up the coast to San Francisco and then taken Interstate 80 through Nevada, Utah, Wyoming, Nebraska, Iowa and Illinois to Detroit — a truly amazing analysis. The most obvious way to go to Canada from California would be north through Oregon and Washington State so why did the truck go to Detroit? Clearly, there was a drug deal going on and knowing the route taken by the truck gave investigators a lead.

Another interesting finding from pollen analysis concerned the use of panga boats by drug smugglers. Pangas are small boats that are powered by outboard motors and can be carried on a trailer towed by a car. These would be loaded with drugs in Mexico and sailed up the west coast of the US where the drugs would be off-loaded and the boats abandoned. Swabbing of the boats collected lots of pollen including that from certain trees that only grow in the mountains in Mexico. The boats were being loaded with drugs at high elevations and then taken by car down to sea level for launching. Knowing this helped the Mexican authorities to locate the distribution centre.

Pollen analysis also helped the CBP to identify the source of marijuana and cocaine bundles that regularly washed up on the coasts of Florida and Texas. Examination showed that many of them were heavily contaminated with fern spores. The density of the spores was such that the drugs had to have come from an area that has a very high density of ferns. This led to Fern Gully, a winding and very scenic stretch of road in Jamaica, as the original source of all of these 'wash ups'.

The distribution of drugs in the US can also be followed

171

by pollen analysis. A batch of five hundred grams of cocaine was seized in a drug raid in New York City. The pollen of tropical plants found in the cocaine indicated that the drug had come from either Bolivia or Colombia where coca plants are grown commercially. Other pollen types that were found came from sub-alpine conifers including Canadian hemlock (*Tsuga canadensis*) and jack pines (*Pinus banksiana*). These two species only grow together in limited regions of Eastern Canada and North-eastern US, suggesting that this was where the cocaine was imported from South America. Because the conifer pollen was in the cocaine itself the shipment must have been opened after its arrival, presumably to be 'cut' with sugar.

A third type of pollen was found in the cocaine shipment and this came from weeds and other plants commonly found growing in vacant lots in the urban slums of New York City. This indicated that when the cocaine reached the city it was again opened and cut further before being packaged for local distribution.

Investigating theft

A European company exported some machinery to a location in Asia. The machinery was packed in wooden crates, and during the voyage the ship stopped in a number of ports where various cargoes were loaded and unloaded. When the wooden crates reached their final destination, the company found only sacks of soil. Investigators determined that somewhere en route the machinery had been stolen and the crates had been refilled with the soil. Where had the switch occurred? Samples of the dirt were sent to a forensic laboratory and examined for pollen. The types of pollen and spores recovered from the soil showed a geographical association with plants normally found in South Africa. Since one of the ports where the ship had stopped was Cape Town, investigators focussed their search for the missing machinery in that city. Several months later, the missing machinery was discovered in a South African warehouse.

A consignment of Scotch whisky was shipped overseas. After it arrived, the shipment was unpacked, but only limestone rocks were present. Because both the country of shipment and the country of destination had ample deposits of limestone, authorities were unsure where the whisky had been illegally removed. Rumours soon spread that the whisky had been removed by local workers after it arrived at its final destination. To confirm or deny these rumours, investigators requested that samples of the limestone be examined in hopes of discovering their source. The resulting analysis revealed an array of fossil pollen that linked the rocks to the country where the whisky had been produced, not the country where it had been sent. This proved that the whisky had been removed before it left Scotland.

Did pollen cause a plane crash?

In December 1989, a private twin-engine plane took off from San Diego airport and headed east. About ninety minutes later it crashed in flames near Ruidoso, New Mexico killing the pilot and his wife. Air accident investigators found no defects in the plane or its engines and concluded that pilot error was to blame for the crash. The wreckage was stored outside in a yard near Ruidoso. About nine months later, attorneys acting for the children of the dead couple ordered their own investigation. It was found that a mass of biological material, mostly pollen, blocked a component of the fuel line called the

B2 elbow. The attorneys filed a lawsuit against the manufacturers of the plane and the fuel control units, claiming that during the flight the engines ingested this material which lodged in the fuel line and caused a loss of power. A simple filter could have prevented the problem had one been fitted.

The defence attorneys called in palynologists to determine if pollen really had been the cause of the crash. Examination of the pollen revealed that it was mainly from two plants, yellow sweet clover (*Melilotus officinalis*) and curlycup gumweed (*Grindelia squarrosa*). Neither of these plants would have been in flower when the crash occurred. Furthermore, the pollen from these plants is relatively heavy because it is transferred from plant to plant by insects. The only pollen that would have been present at the cruising height of the plane would be the very light grains produced by wind pollinated plants. Finally, when the pollen grains from the B2 elbow were put on some nutrient jelly they started to grow, i.e. they were viable. When the plane crashed, it burned for several hours and the temperature would have exceeded one thousand degrees centigrade. This would have killed any pollen that was present. So, where had the pollen come from?

Detailed examination of the pollen in the B2 elbow revealed the presence of tiny hairs. These were identified as coming from a leafcutter bee. These bees live in pre-existing tunnels and feed their offspring pollen. One of them had taken up residence in the B2 elbow during the spring and summer when the engine parts were lying in the open yard. The attorneys for the family lost their case.

Postscript

It is estimated that there are about one thousand palynologists in the whole world and more than half of these are employed by the petroleum industry. Many others work in the field of archaeology to uncover the lives of our early ancestors. The number of individuals that are involved in forensic palynology can be counted on two hands, and perhaps just one. An amazing statistic when you consider the prevalence of violent crime and the successes recounted above.

WHAT WOOD CAN TELL US

Wood can be found at crime scenes in many forms: as a murder weapon, as material to hide a body, as trace evidence from forced entry or vandalism or as splinters from an explosion. Although there are about eighteen thousand different woody species in the world, only a few hundred are in commercial use. In some ways this makes wood identification simpler than pollen identification but it can be difficult to identify a piece of wood as coming from a particular species: often the best that can be done is to identify down to the level of the genus of plant. As with pollen, when an unusual piece of wood is found, i.e. one that is not in commercial use, it can be particularly incriminating. For example, in two separate murder cases in the US, pool cues were used as the weapon. Wood fragments were found embedded in the victims' heads and on the suspects. In both cases, the cues were made from unusual tropical woods and this helped to secure convictions.

The detection of the killer of baby Lindbergh was described in chapter one and this case was the first time that forensic wood analysis was used in a criminal investigation. In a murder case in the US state of Georgia, a woman's body was found in some woods covered with debris that had been sourced nearby. Among the debris were two red-painted posts made of oak. These were thought to belong to the suspect who was the husband of the victim. When the victim's house was searched, a red smudge was found on a piece of yellow pine. The chemical analysis of this paint matched that of the red posts but this did not prove conclusively that the posts had ever been in the victim's house. However, there were some tiny wood fibres stuck to the red smudge on the piece of yellow pine. Microscopic analysis showed these to be from the oak posts and this provided a direct link to the murder scene.

In a case in Texas the murderer tried to dispose of the victim's body in a bonfire but without success. Detectives investigating the case discovered that the prime suspect had taken some logs to a party about the time the victim went missing. They collected ten logs from the murder scene and four logs from the party fireplace and sent them off to a laboratory specialising in dating trees by analysis of tree rings. Just as in the Lindbergh case, they wanted to know if all the logs came from the same tree. However, the logs were all from mesquite (*Prosopis glanduola*). This tree does not form the familiar growth rings because of the erratic nature of tree growth in the arid desert from which it originates. So, scientists used a very specialist analytical technique which generates a chemical fingerprint that reflects the soil type and underlying geology where the tree was grown. This showed that all the logs had identical amounts of carbon, magnesium, silicon, aluminium, calcium, manganese, iron, titanium and nitrogen. If all the logs did not come from the same tree then they had to come from trees that were growing very close together. Once again there was a link between suspect and crime scene.

In one notable case, wood analysis was able to prove that someone was innocent of a crime. A young girl went missing in one of Utah's National Parks and her body was never found.

However, near where she went missing there was an aspen tree and on it was carved 'Ted Bundy 78'. This discovery caused a furore because Ted Bundy was known to be a serial kidnapper, rapist and killer. Had Bundy carved his own name on the tree or had someone else done it to incriminate him? The piece of tree carrying Bundy's name was cut out and sent to an expert in bark anatomy. He found that where the letters had been carved the tree had responded by laying down what is known as wound periderm. There were eight layers of this periderm so the letters had been carved eight years previously. As Bundy was in prison eight years earlier, he certainly had not carved his name on the tree. However, this was of little consequence because he subsequently went to the electric chair for all of his other crimes.

Analysis of wound damage also has been used to establish time of death. In this case a skeleton was found beneath a magnolia tree and a piece of shirt sleeve was found around a branch about twenty feet above the ground. The shirt-sleeve had caused a constriction in the branch and by counting the number of tree rings in the constricted and non-constricted areas, it was possible to give the time of death as being about five years earlier.

Wood analysis has also been used in civil cases involving insurance claims. Investigators at the scene of a double fatality found a piece of wood embedded in the wreckage of a car. Relatives of the deceased believed that the piece of wood was responsible for the accident and, if this were true, would have a significant impact on the amount that the insurance company would pay out. When the piece of wood was examined by a wood expert, he was able to identify the species and size of the tree from which it had come. When the expert visited the scene of the accident, he was able to pinpoint the exact origin of the wood fragment. The height of the damage indicated to him that the car was airborne when it grazed the tree. So, the wood fragment was a consequence of the accident and not the cause of it.

Identifying protected wood species

The Convention on International Trade in Endangered Species of Wild Fauna and Flora (CITES) is a multilateral treaty dating from 1973 whose aim is to ensure that international trade in specimens of wild animals and plants does not threaten the survival of the species in the wild. The use of the word 'trade' in this context does not refer to commercial or non-commercial uses but the movement of specimens across international borders. In the case of plants, nearly thirty thousand species are covered by CITES but only a small number of these are trees. Each protected species or population is included in one of three lists, known as appendices, and these lists are reviewed tri-annually.

CITES Appendix I lists species that are threatened with extinction and are or may be affected by trade. Commercial trade in these species is illegal unless exceptional circumstances apply and a special permit has been obtained. Not surprisingly, the list includes commercially-valuable trees such as Brazilian mahogany (*Swietenia macrophylla*) and Brazilian rosewood (*Dahlbergia nigrans*) so beloved of the makers of furniture and musical instruments. The second appendix covers species that are not necessarily threatened with extinction, but may become so unless trade in specimens of such species is subject to strict regulation, in order to avoid utilisation incompatible with the survival of the species in the wild. Appendix III contains species that are protected in at least one country which has asked other CITES signatories for assistance in controlling trade.

A listing generally means that trade of the raw wood, either in log, board or veneer form is restricted. For some species, the restriction is even greater and includes finished products made with the protected wood, e.g. guitars made of Brazilian Rosewood. In these instances, it is illegal to take such items across international borders without a proper export permit. If the owner believes that the wood or wood product was harvested or made before the CITES listing, then they need written proof.

A major problem for customs agents is being able to identify illegal species among lumber imports especially if it is accompanied by false documentation. Even wood analysts can have trouble identifying particular species with the aid of a microscope so what hope is there for the hapless custom official? However, just as with the narcotics trade, the black market price of timber covered by CITES is very high and there are criminal gangs behind its illegal movement. This is driving the development of new analytical techniques that can be used to identify not just the species of tree that the wood came from but also where in the world that the source tree grew. Fortunately, the most trafficked wood covered by CITES is rosewood and this is relatively easy to identify visually. In Thailand the authorities make one seizure every day and in Singapore in 2014 they made the biggest seizure of any item covered by CITES. This was a shipment of thirty thousand logs with a value of £18 million.

PEN PORTRAIT: THE LEADING PLAYERS IN FORENSIC BOTANY

The forensic botany community is a small one and all the members know one another, although only a few of them have international status. Dallas Mildenhall in New Zealand pioneered the use of forensic palynology, first in his home country and then elsewhere in the world. Despite its size, the US has just one full-time forensic palynologist: Andrew Laurence who was trained by another expert forensic palynologist, Vaughn Bryant. Then there is Patricia Wiltshire in the UK who is not just a forensic palynologist but a forensic botanist. Finally, in terms of wood analysis, there is no organisation to compare with the USDA Forest Products Laboratory in Madison, Wisconsin.

Dallas Mildenhall

Mildenhall undoubtedly is the king of forensic palynology having worked on over four hundred cases ranging from theft, rape and murder to counterfeit pharmaceuticals and stolen art. He was born and raised in New Zealand's North Island in the region around the national capital, Wellington. The son of an import/export merchant, he was motivated to do science by an inspirational college teacher. At university he studied botany and geology and yet, when he graduated, he had never seen a pollen grain under the microscope. After graduation, he took a job as a geologist with the government's Department of Scientific and Industrial Research and never left, although the part that he joined now is GNS Science. It was here that he developed his skills as a palynologist but in biostratigraphy (determining the age of geological strata) and paleoclimatology (inferring past climatic conditions from analysis of vegetation in geological strata). Oil companies use this kind of information to try and find new oil deposits.

His first foray into forensic palynology came in 1983 in the Kirsa Jensen case (page 161). Although nobody was found guilty of the murder of Kirsa, Mildenhall's work on pollen analysis gave police a clear lead to the principal suspect. Fifteen years later Mildenhall was again called in by the police, this time to help investigate the murder of fifteen-year-old Kirsty Bentley. She had taken her dog for a walk and never returned to her home near Christchurch. Several weeks later her body was found twenty-five miles away in Rakai Gorge. Mildenhall's work produced no leads and nobody was ever charged with her murder. These two cases still trouble Mildenhall today.

When Mellory Manning was murdered in 2008 (page 164) the detective in charge of the investigation was Greg Williams. He had worked with Mildenhall on the Kirsty Bentley case and despite the lack of success he was still bullish about the potential of forensic palynology. He was right to be so because pollen analysis identified the site of the murder and provided the link to the perpetrator. This case also made Mildenhall's reputation. From then on, assisting in criminal cases became a significant part of his workload and he has been an expert witness in criminal cases in Australia and the UK, as well as in his native New Zealand. Although he is in his seventies, he still undertakes forensic palynology for there is nobody to replace him. His skills are unique.

Mildenhall is on record as saying that if you have committed a crime and the police suspect that you have done it then never deny having been at the scene where the crime was committed, for pollen analysis will find you out. What you should do is admit to having been at the scene but deny committing the crime which puts the onus on the police. Would-be criminals take note!

Patricia Wiltshire

Wiltshire was born in Monmouthshire in South Wales. When she was a young child, she suffered from a double dose of whooping cough and measles. This left her with a chronic weak chest which led to repeated respiratory infections. Consequently, she spent a lot of time in bed and this led to a rather unconventional education: reading encyclopaedias. She taught herself all sorts of things from these books ranging from knitting to music. After leaving school, she worked as a medical laboratory technician but was repulsed by animal experimentation. So, at the age of twenty-eight years she began studying botany at King's College in London. After graduation, she stayed on as a lecturer in plant and microbial ecology before moving to a post in the Institute of Archaeology at University College, London. Whilst there she set up a course in Forensic Archaeological Science.

In 1995, an event occurred that was to completely change her career path. Hertfordshire Police contacted Kew Gardens looking for assistance in a murder case. Kew Gardens was unable to help but suggested that Wiltshire might be able to do so. This proved to be the case: Wiltshire was not only able to show that the suspects had been in the field where the body had been found, but also was able to show where the body had been long after it had been removed (p167). That case made her name in police circles and from then on, she was called in on more and more police investigations including some very high-profile UK murder cases, such as the Soham ones (p148), Sarah Payne, Milly Dowler and the serial murder of prostitutes in Ipswich. In 2006 alone, she worked on twenty-five cases involving missing persons, rape and murder.

In 2006 Wiltshire met, and later married, David Hawksworth who was an eminent mycologist working at the University of Madrid. Just as flowering plants produce pollen as part of the reproductive process, fungi produce spores. The spores from different fungi have different morphologies, in the same way that pollen grains do, and can be used forensically. Hawksworth and Wiltshire have put their joint expertise to good use. In one case in Dundee, the body of a murdered woman was found on the planted periphery of a busy roundabout. A suspect was apprehended and his footwear yielded a similar botanical and fungal profile to that obtained from the crime scene and the victim's clothing. In her biography (Traces, 535 Press, 2019), Wiltshire provides details of her laboratory methods and a number of other notable cases not covered in this book.

Like Dallas Mildenhall, Wiltshire is in her seventies and there is nobody else in the UK with her level of expertise in forensic botany. When she is not involved at crime scenes she can be found at home fostering stray cats and playing Chopin and Mozart on the piano. Or she might be working in the local antique shop putting her knowledge of 17th and 18th century oak furniture to work. A lady with these skills who is in her seventies and only five feet tall sounds like an archetypal Agatha Christie detective.

Vaughn Bryant and Andrew Laurence

Vaughn Bryant's early life was spent in various parts of the world but when he was a teenager the family finally settled in Houston. After high school, he enrolled at the University of Texas at Austin where he majored in geography. He chose to study anthropology for his master's degree and to pay his way through his course he took a job as a palynology assistant. When he started this job he did not even know what palynology was but soon became obsessed with it. Later, as an anthropologist at Texas A&M university he established his own pollen laboratory.

In 1975 the US Department of Agriculture paid Bryant to help them track down counterfeit honey (see next chapter) which was not coming from where the sellers claimed. He figured out where each honey sample came from by looking at the pollen grains in it, because these reflect the plants on which the bees were feeding. Although the money for doing this was not substantial, it did help to pay for his laboratory. Academic scientists are always struggling to get sufficient funding so Bryant began giving lectures about the uses of palynology to various federal agencies. One of these lectures was to the Sheriff's Association of Texas and this led to his first criminal case.

The sheriff of Nolan County brought Bryant the clothes of an unknown man who had been stabbed twenty-one times and left under a mesquite bush. It was believed that the man had been killed over drugs so the police were focussing their search towards the Mexican border. After looking at the pollen on the clothes, Bryant told the sheriff to look around Kansas City. Eventually there was huge drug raid in Kansas City but Bryant never knew if his work had any connection with it. Nevertheless, this first case led to other cases around the US.

The CIA came calling after the events of 9/11. Soon he started receiving backpacks, scarves, parts of bombs, bits of rope, etc. with no information about their source. Identifying the source was his job. On one occasion, he was sent a thirty-six-inch shoelace and asked where it had been. He found more than five thousand grains of pollen on it and was able to say conclusively that it had been to Iran and Iraq. However, after Osama Bin Laden was tracked down and killed, the CIA had no further need for Bryant's services - but the FBI and the Department of Homeland Security did! They wanted him to help combat drug trafficking along the US-Mexico border and they wanted him full-time. But Bryant loves teaching and so he trained one of his students, Andrew Laurence, to do the job.

Andrew Laurence is the only full-time forensic palynologist in the whole of the United States and he works for the Department of Customs and Border Protection. He grew up in Cleveland, Ohio and originally had aspirations to be a pilot in the US Navy. This career was ruled out when he got injured at the Merchant Marine Academy and he switched to studying archaeology at Kent State University. After graduating, he moved to Texas A&M University to study for his PhD under Vaughn Bryant. Bryant recognised that Laurence had the particular skills and obsessiveness that a good forensic palynologist requires. Today, Laurence is the only internationally recognised forensic palynologist in the world who is under sixty years of age, which is rather worrying!

PART Five:
A MISCELLANEY OF
AUTHENTICITY ISSUES

ARE YOU TAKING WHAT YOU THINK YOU ARE TAKING?

A book published in 1820 caused a scandal, first in Britain but later in Germany. It was called 'A Treatise on Adulterations of Food and Culinary Poisons' and had a sub-title taken from the New Testament Book of Kings: 'There is death in the pot'. One thousand copies of the book were sold within a month of its publication, which shows its importance at the time. A second run was printed the same year and a German edition was published two years later. The author of the book was a German chemist, Fredrick Accum, who had served an apprenticeship as an apothecary after coming to London in 1793.

In the book, Accum gave many examples of unscrupulous practices such as bulking out sacks of coffee with sheep dung and adulterating exhausted coffee grounds with roasted peas, chicory or turnip. Bread loaves were extended with mashed potatoes, plaster of Paris and sawdust whilst strychnine was added to beer instead of hops. Some of the other practices Accum described were more worrying, such as colouring red cheese with mercuric sulphide and red lead. One of the most damning sentences in the whole book is:

'The man who robs a fellow subject of a few shillings on the high-way, is sentenced to death; while he who distributes a slow poison to a whole community, escapes punishment'.

To make his point more clearly, Accum included at the end of each chapter the names of merchants who had been caught adulterating foodstuffs. Not surprisingly, there were many threats made against him following publication of the book.

In 1821 Accum was caught up in a scandal and a lawsuit and he returned to his native Germany. Thirty years later, a London physician called Edward Hill Hassall began his own campaign against food adulteration. In this task he was helped by Henry Letherby who was London's Medical Officer of Health. Their work led to the Food Adulteration Act of 1860 which was revised and extended in 1872. It also led to the establishment of public analysts. These are scientists in the United Kingdom and Ireland whose principal task is to ensure the safety and correct description of food by testing for compliance with legislation. The difficulties faced by public analysts, difficulties that remain today, were highlighted by the writer Charles Kingsley in his classic book 'The Water Babies', when he wrote:

'...those who invent poisons for little children and sell them at wakes, fairs and tuck shops. Dr Letheby and Dr Hassall cannot catch them all...'

This is a reference to confectionary being coloured with red lead, mercuric sulphide and copper arsenite!

The problems described above were not confined to food, for substitution of one substance with another was rife within medicine. Until the second half of the 20th century almost all drugs were derived from plants. As apothecary Thomas Johnson wrote in 1632:

'One or other druggists, to the great peril of their patients, lays himself open to the mockery of women who deal in roots.

These women know only too well the unskilled and thrust upon them brazenly what they please or what they will. For the doctor relies on the druggist and the druggist on a greedy and dirty woman with the audacity and the capacity to impose anything on him. So it often happens that the patient's safety depends on the herbal knowledge of an ignorant and crafty woman.'

The problem of fake herbs was compounded by the fact that many of them were not native to Britain so the apothecaries did not know what the genuine material should look like. Quinine came from the bark of the cinchona tree but this grew in South America, so an unscrupulous dealer could pass off anything as cinchona bark, particularly if it had been pulverised.

To minimise the use of the wrong plants in medicine various authorities established physic gardens where doctors could learn to recognise different plants. The first of these were established in 1334 in Venice and Salerno and another four were developed in Italy over the next two hundred years. Zurich established one in 1560, Paris in 1570 and Leiden in 1577. It was 1633 before the first one was established in England in Oxford. By this time, the London apothecaries had persuaded King James I to let them split from the Grocer's Company and form the Society of Apothecaries. In 1673 the Society leased three acres of land in Chelsea and built their own garden which today is the Chelsea Physic Garden. Although apothecaries could be taught to recognise whole plants this was of little use in determining the authenticity of parts of plants such as roots or bark. Following the development of the compound microscope in the 17th century the training of apothecaries included identifying plant materials from their morphological and microscopic structure pharmacognosy. In addition, just as with food, various laws were passed which governed the quality of raw materials and finished products that were sold as drugs.

Do you know what you are eating?

The World Health Organization defines a counterfeit product as one that is mislabelled deliberately and fraudulently with respect to its identity or source. The food industry is awash with counterfeit products today. Ten times more Basmati rice is sold than is grown. Hard or Durum wheat is substituted with bread wheat. Italian authorities recently discovered that the country was importing very large quantities of olive oil from Spain and re-labelling it as having been made in Italy. Daffodil stamens are dyed and sold as saffron, the most expensive spice in the world. The scale of the problem is illustrated by Operation Opson VII which ran in sixty-seven countries from December 2017 to March 2018. This resulted in the seizure of three thousand six hundred and twenty tonnes and 9.7 million litres of counterfeit or sub-standard food and beverages - and this is estimated to be less than 1% of what is in the supply chain!

Go to the supermarket and a jar of basic honey will cost 99p. In the delicatessen a jar of single source honey, such as that from heather, will cost £6 and the same amount of genuine New Zealand Manuka honey will cost £15. Single sourced honey originates from a single flower type and takes on the unique flavour and characteristics of that blossom. In order to capture a single source of nectar the beekeeper is restricted in where he can put his hives of honeybees. This is what makes single source honey expensive. But an unscrupulous producer can increase their profit margin by adulterating a single source honey with basic or multifloral honey and today, honey is the world's third most faked food. The problem is particularly acute in Europe because it cannot produce enough to meet demand and sources much of what it consumes from China.

Honey is an unprocessed product and should contain pollen from the plants that the bees visited when searching for nectar. A product that is sold as honey but does not contain pollen is not the genuine thing and there is much of this fake material on the market. A study of over two thousand samples from EU member states found over 20% were not as claimed. Consequently, pollen analysis of honey (melissopalynology) is an essential tool for routine verification of the claimed geographic and floral origin of honey samples, particularly in the European Union. However, the technique is not without its problems. Apart from the difficulty in finding experienced palynologists, what proportion of pollen in a honey sample must come from a single species of plant in order for the honey to be labelled as 'single source'?

Eucalyptus trees are native to Australia but have been planted widely, and often become naturalised, in southern Asia, South America, Africa and many countries within the Mediterranean basin. These trees reward pollinators with very heavy nectar and/or pollen production and so are important nectar sources for honey bees. Given that a honey bee will visit other plants, even when the density of eucalyptus trees is very high, what proportion of the pollen in a unifloral Eucalyptus honey should come from that tree? Based on an examination of two hundred and eight samples from the Mediterranean region, the International Honey Commission declared that it should have a minimum of 83% of its pollen from Eucalyptus and the average level should be 95%.

Australia is a major producer of honey and exports nearly five thousand tonnes, much of it unifloral Eucalyptus honey. However, seven out of twenty (35%) of samples labelled as such were rejected outright when pollen analysis was done by European mellisopalynologists. Of the remaining thirteen samples, Eucalyptus pollen was present but below 80% of total pollen and in two cases less than 50%. It turns out that the Australian producers were not indulging in wholescale fraud. Only a few different species of Eucalyptus are found in the Mediterranean region making it easy to identify the pollen from them. In Australia there are eight hundred species of Eucalyptus, of which dozens are used by beekeepers. This means that the palynological criteria developed for European Eucalyptus honeys cannot be applied to honey originating from Australia — or anywhere else for that matter.

Of all the honeys that can be bought, the most prized and most expensive is Mānuka honey. This is produced by bees foraging on the Mānuka or tea tree (*Leptospermum scoparium*) which grows uncultivated throughout New Zealand. It is renowned for its rich flavour and for the presence of Unique Mānuka Factor (UMF). All honey has varying levels of antibacterial activity due to the presence of hydrogen peroxide, but Mānuka honey has additional antibacterial activity due to the presence of a chemical called methylglyoxal. This is marketed as UMF. Pure Mānuka honey is rated from 5+ to 20+. The higher the UMF rating, the more methylglyoxal the honey contains and the higher the price. This makes it a target for fraudsters: only one thousand seven hundred tonnes of Manuka honey are produced each year but over ten thousand tonnes are sold globally including one thousand eight hundred tonnes in the UK. To combat this fraud, the New Zealand government has produced a set of tests for authenticity that includes methylglyoxal content as well as detection of pollen and DNA from *Leptospermum scoparium*.

DNA testing and the Barcode of Life

Imagine that you have gone to the supermarket and paid a premium for Basmati in the expectation of tucking in to a helping of lightly-perfumed, fluffy rice along with your lamb bhuna or chicken tikka. Expectation turns to disappointment when you end up with a saucepan of sticky rice. Unless you are of Indian or Pakistani origin you will assume that the problem was caused by incorrect cooking rather than adulteration with cheap long-grain rice. Surveys done on products sold as Basmati in British supermarkets showed that nearly 50% had significant adulteration and some did not even contain the variety listed on the packet. But how does one determine if rice grains originate from the foothills of the Himalaya as true Basmati does? The answer lies in DNA testing.

Just as 'DNA fingerprinting', more correctly DNA profiling, has been used to identify criminals from materials left at a crime scene, the technique can be used to combat food fraud. Analysis of DNA has been used widely to determine the authenticity of different food products including detecting adulteration or substitution of Basmati, differentiating the species of citrus fruits that have been used to produce orange juice, detecting the adulteration or substitution of Durum wheat with bread wheat and determining if premium priced potato varieties (e.g. King Edward) have been substituted with much cheaper varieties (e.g. Ambo).

Conventional DNA testing is very useful if one wishes to determine if a particular species of plant is present in a sample and, if so, how much is present. It does not matter if the test material is intact plants or pulverised tissue: the DNA still can be analysed. However, if one detects that other material is present that should not be there, then identifying this extraneous material can be extremely difficult. At least, it was before the advent of the Barcode of Life. The barcode in this case refers to a standardised short piece of DNA about 400–800 base pairs ('building blocks') long. These pieces of DNA are easily recoverable from test samples and their sequence determined. A single sequence of DNA from the cytochrome C oxidase 1 gene can be used to identify tissue from any animal. For plant material to be identified unambiguously it is necessary to sequence DNA from one or more of four genes (*rbc*L, *mat*K, *trn*H-*psb*A and ITS).

The beauty of the Barcode of Life is that it enables investigators to identify any plant material found during a criminal investigation. Imagine that some leaves have been found at a crime scene and that these do not match the leaves on any of the surrounding trees. You take the leaves to a forensic botanist but they are not able to identify them as they have never seen such leaves before. So, you go to a botanic garden like Kew and they might be able to recognise the leaves although this could take some time. Alternatively, you can extract some DNA from a tiny portion of the leaves and sequence it. You then look up the sequence in the international reference database and, hey presto, you have your identification. Then you can ask a botanist if the appearance of the leaves matches those kept in the herbaria of botanic gardens — a much simpler process. Imagine how much easier it would have been to identify the remains of Calabar beans found in the stomach of 'Adam' (described in chapter nine) if this technique had been available at the time. As noted on page 180, it can be extremely difficult to identify tropical hardwoods which is essential in the fight against illegal logging. Here, again, DNA barcoding can be very useful.

Is that medicine what you think it is?

Herbal products are widely used in both the developing and the developed nations to promote good health and as a substitute for conventional pharmaceuticals in the treatment of disease. Examples of products used in the West include ginseng (promote good health), ginkgo (improve circulation), hypericin from St John's wort (to treat depression), the black cohosh (to treat menopausal symptoms), and Echinacea (to prevent colds). More than one thousand companies are involved in the manufacture of herbal products and the total market is worth one hundred billion dollars and growing at 6–10% per annum. A market this size translates into hundreds of millions of customers — but are they buying what they think that they are buying? Has there been product adulteration or substitution with species of lower or even no market value? This is an important question because we saw in part two of this book that most plants produce one or more potent toxins, of which only a few have been used to deliberately poison someone.

With the advent of DNA barcoding it is possible to sample an herbal product and ask if the labelled ingredient is present and if any other undeclared plant species are present. Professor Steven Newmaster at the University of Guelph in Canada is one of the leaders in the field and his findings give serious cause for concern. He surveyed forty-four herbal products on the North American market and found that one third of them did not contain the plant species indicated. He also detected the use of undeclared fillers such as rice, alfalfa (lucerne), soybean and wheat. Fillers are cheap plant products with no known beneficial health effects and in some of the herbal products these were the only plant materials present. Such fillers could be problematic for people with grass allergies or gluten intolerance.

A group at University College, London tested a sample of thirty ginkgo products and found that eight of them (27%) contained no ginkgo. They also found that one milk thistle (*Silybum marianum*) product, which is sold as a treatment for cirrhosis, jaundice and hepatitis contained no trace of the plant. Every product that turned out to have no active ingredient had been purchased from online retailers!

Whereas some herbal products sampled by Newmaster contained no active ingredient others contained substitute plant materials. One product was labelled as St John's wort (*Hypericum perforatum*) but contained *Senna alexandria* instead. This is of great concern because senna is an over the counter (OTC) medicine for treating constipation. It should not be taken long term because it can cause chronic diarrhoea and liver damage. Other products that were tested were contaminated with feverfew (*Parthenium hysterophorus*) which is used as an herbal remedy for migraine. Again, this is a substance that should not be taken chronically because it has numerous undesirable side effects. Other products were contaminated with black walnut (*Juglans nigra*) which could be a risk for consumers with nut allergies.

Over the past twenty-five years the use of traditional Chinese medicine (TCM) has become increasingly popular in Europe, the USA and Australasia. TCM differs from Western herbal medicine in a number of key respects. Western herbal medicines usually consist of a single plant species. By contrast, patients receiving TCM are given preparations made from parts of plants rather than the purified active ingredient. Furthermore, they are often given mixtures of several herbs with the function of some of them being to reduce the toxicity or increase the potency of other herbs in the mixture. Also, the processing of the plants is very important in TCM. Basic processing includes washing, drying or slicing the plant material to clean the herbs and improve storage properties. Additional processing such as stir-frying, boiling or steaming is used to modify therapeutic effects, remove toxic materials and alter bioavailability or preserve active ingredients. All this makes checking the authenticity of TCM products much more difficult but scientists have been able to apply barcoding. For example, some of the adulterants found in Chinese herbal products include *Adenostyles alliariae* (causes serious liver damage), *Illicium anisatum* (contains neurotoxic substances) as well as our old friends *Aconitum* (chapter eight) and *Datura* (chapter six). However, not all cases of serious illness are caused by counterfeit products.

Botanist Christine Leon was working in the Medical Toxicology Unit at Guy's Hospital in London in 1998 when she received a query from a specialist in renal medicine. He had a female Caucasian patient who was progressing rapidly to end-stage renal failure. The only medicine this patient was taking, and had been for two years, was a Chinese herbal remedy (Mu Tong) for eczema. The clinician wanted to know if the herbal medicine had caused the problem. Then, one week later, a clinician in another hospital also contacted Christine about a Caucasian patient in renal failure who for six years had been taking a Chinese herbal tea for eczema. Was the juxtaposition of the two cases more than a coincidence?

Mu Tong is the name given to preparations from the stems of *Aristolochia manshuriensis* (Guan Mu Tong), as well as two species of *Clematis* (Chuan Mu Tong) and two of *Akebia* (San Ye Mu Tong and Wu Ye Mu Tong). Unlike *Clematis* and *Akebia*, *Aristolochia* species contain aristolochic acid that is a known nephrotoxin (causes kidney damage) and carcinogen. Christine suspected that *Aristolochia manshuriensis* erroneously had been administered instead of *Clematis*. This was confirmed by chemical analysis that showed that the herbal preparations taken by the two patients contained aristolochic acid. Had it not been for the presence of this acid the identification of the problem would have been very difficult for there were no plant reference materials from which to work, not even at Kew Gardens.

Numerous initiatives are underway to try and combat the spread of counterfeit herbal medicines and the inadvertent use of the wrong plant species. Christine Leon, working with Chinese colleagues, has established at Kew Gardens a reference collection of herbal materials used in TCM. Steven Newmaster has initiated a database of DNA barcodes but with over one thousand two hundred plants used in Western herbal medicine, it will take him some time to complete this task. The problem that he faces is not generating the barcodes but getting authentic specimens (voucher specimens) of the relevant plants. Finally, the American Botanical Council, the American Herbal Pharmacopoeia and the National Center for Natural Product Research has established the Botanical Adulterants Prevention Program. The fact that these initiatives are needed should be a reminder to readers that herbal medicines are not safer than chemically-purified drugs.

DETERMINING THE AUTHENTICITY OF ARTEFACTS

It was particularly dry in China's Shaanxi province in March 1974 and so a group of peasants decided to dig a well to water the crops of their cooperative farm. On the first day, the digging went well but on the second day, hard red earth was hit. On the third day, Yang Zhifa's hoe encountered some terracotta and he told his workmate that they probably were digging on the site of an old kiln. His workmate advised that they dig carefully so that they would preserve any old jars that might be present and which they could take home for their own use. As the digging continued, the peasants uncovered the shoulders and torso of what turned out to be a headless statue. A decade earlier Yang had uncovered three kneeling archers made from terracotta so he knew what he was looking at.

The farmers started digging up more statues until they had enough to load onto three hand-drawn carts that were then taken to the Lintong District Museum a few kilometres away. Yang was not sure if the museum would be interested in the terracotta but thought the journey was worth the effort. He was in luck. The peasants got paid ten yuan per cart, i.e. a total of thirty yuan, and were ecstatic because ten yuan was the annual salary of a peasant in rural areas. The archaeologist at the museum, Zhao Kangmin, had recognised that something exciting had just been delivered. He started sorting through the terracotta and three days later he had two terracotta warriors, each about six feet tall. They had been crafted during the Qin dynasty in the third century BC.

Zhao was very nervous about the discovery of the warriors, for in 1974 China was still in the grip of Chairman Mao's Cultural Revolution. This was a time when the dreaded Red Guards sought to destroy old traditions to 'purify' society. The relics might be smashed for political reasons. Zhao decided to keep the discovery a secret but word leaked out and was soon known to the Communist Party leadership. Fortunately, they decided to excavate the site and within a few months more than five hundred warriors had been found. Eventually the scale of the terracotta army became clear: eight thousand soldiers, one hundred and thirty chariots, six hundred and seventy horses plus a number of entertainers such as dancers, acrobats and musicians. The warriors had been placed in battle formation, ready to defend China's first emperor in the afterlife. The find is ranked as one of the greatest discoveries of the 20th century and the collection of figures is one of the greatest archaeological sites in the world.

It is believed that the heads, arms, legs and torsos were created separately and then assembled. After assembly, clay was applied to the surface of the sculptures so that artists could model the faces and hairdos individually. In this way every figure could be made to look different. So, we know how they were made but where were they made? One way to try and answer this question is to do pollen analysis. The pollen obtained from the terracotta horses was mostly from trees and was similar to that in the local soil. By contrast, the pollen from the warriors themselves came mostly from herbaceous plants that do not grow locally to the site. One thought is that the scale of the task of making the complete assemblage was so great that it was done at more than one site. The horses have relatively fragile legs, which would be prone to damage, and are much bigger and heavier than the warriors. Therefore, it would make sense to produce the horses locally. The warriors, which were assembled from individual parts, could be made elsewhere.

Are fabric-based artefacts what they are claimed to be?

The Gondar Hanging in the Royal Ontario Museum is the largest known tablet-woven textile in the world measuring seventeen feet by seven feet. It supposedly dated from the late 17th or early 18th century and originally hung in one of Ethiopia's Christian churches, but could it have been a fake? The Hanging is made from spun heavy silk and consists of three vertical panels. Woven into each panel is a series of motifs with iconography relating to the Ethiopian church and the royal family. By 1993 the Hanging was very dirty and the silk fibres were beginning to deteriorate and so was sent to the Canadian Conservation Institute for restoration and cleaning. It was decided that this would be a good time to try and determine the authenticity as well.

It was hoped that any pollen trapped between the weave of the Hanging, along with the associated packing materials, might confirm its origin as being Ethiopian. Studies of the pollen contents of the Hanging revealed that many of the originating plants could be traced to probable Canadian sources as would be expected. However, a few of the pollen types recovered, including *Justicia* (water willow) and *Olea chrysophylla* (olive), were not from native Canadian plants, nor from plants that might have been grown as ornamentals in Canada. Both *Justicia* and *Olea* are plants that are common in the flora of Ethiopia, and can also be found growing throughout the Mediterranean and North African regions. Therefore, the pollen evidence confirmed the probable origin of the Gondar Hanging as being Ethiopian, or from a similar country in Northern Africa, and the museum was very happy.

The Shroud of Turin or Turin Shroud is a length of linen cloth bearing the negative image of a man who is alleged to be Jesus of Nazareth. It is kept in the royal chapel of the Cathedral of Saint John the Baptist in Turin, northern Italy. The cloth itself is believed by some to be the burial shroud that Jesus was wrapped in when he was buried after crucifixion. Its authenticity has never been proven and radiocarbon dating of a sample of the shroud material suggests that it was made around 1390 AD. The Sudarium of Oviedo, or Shroud of Oviedo, is a bloodstained piece of cloth measuring thirty-three by twenty-one inches kept in the Cámara Santa of the Cathedral of San Salvador, Oviedo, Spain. The Sudarium, or sweat cloth in Latin, is thought to be the cloth that was wrapped around the head of Jesus Christ after he died as described in the New Testament book of John. Radiocarbon dating suggests that it was made between 570 and 700 AD.

Both shrouds have been subjected to intensive analysis by experts from many different disciplines to try and better understand their origins. In 1999, scientists from the Hebrew University of Jerusalem detailed a comprehensive analysis of pollen that they had taken from the Turin Shroud. This work was complemented by work in the US involving a sophisticated analysis of imprints of plants and flowers on the cloth itself. The Israeli palynologists reported a high density of pollen from *Gundelia tournefortii*, a thistle that has bloomed for millennia in present-day Israel between March and May, i.e. a period that encompasses Easter. The US study identified 'shadows' of this thistle near the image of the man's shoulder and speculated that this might be the plant used for the crown of thorns that was placed on Jesus' head. Two pollen grains identical to those identified as being from *G. tournefortii* also were found on the Sudarium of Oviedo.

Another plant seen in a clear image on the Shroud is *Zygophyllum dumosum* which is identifiable because of its unusual leaf morphology. Other plant images have been tentatively identified as coming from *Capparis aegyptia* and *Cistus creticus*. The three plants, *G. tournefortii*, *Z. dumosum* and *C. creticus*, only co-exist in the Jerusalem-Hebron area of present-day Israel. Plants of *C. aegyptia* are native to Judean Desert and Dead Sea valley. A re-examination of the pollen data by a Spanish palynologist suggested that pollen thought to come from *G. tournefortii* actually came from a species of *Helichrysum*. This deserves two comments. First, as noted earlier, palynologists seldom can identify pollen down to the level of the species. Second, *Helichrysum* is the source of a high-quality oil that was used to anoint bodies.

So, what can we conclude from the studies described above? If we accept the age of the Turin Shroud based on radiocarbon dating — and there is no reason not to do so — then the images on it are unlikely to be sophisticated forgeries. The most likely series of events is that a body was placed on the cloth along with various flowering plants. Next, the body was anointed with oil which, at the time, almost certainly would have come from one or more plants. The cloth then was folded over the body or wrapped around it and this started the process that resulted in image formation. Based on the plant and pollen studies the wrapping of the body could have happened in what is present-day Israel and we can speculate that the shroud was taken to Italy during the Crusades. The body was that of a man but, based on radiocarbon dating, would not be that of Jesus.

Mis-labelling of a museum specimen

At the natural history museum in Marseille, France, a rare lizard had been on display for years. Information with the display stated that the lizard had been collected during a hunting expedition in New Zealand during the late 1800's. Although no living specimen of this lizard had ever been found in New Zealand, the possibility did exist that the lizard might have been captured in New Zealand and had been one of the last members of its species. A forensic pollen analysis of the dust found inside the stuffed lizard indicated it had probably been mounted in Europe. None of the pollen or spores found inside the lizard were types that would link it to New Zealand, strongly suggesting that this was not its country of origin.

The authenticity of wooden artefacts

A French antique chest was sold at auction. Later, the chest was tested to see if it was authentic. One of the tests was a forensic examination of the dirt and dust trapped inside each of the drawer's small keyholes. To accomplish this test, the lock was removed and the dirt and wood shavings trapped in the lock's corners were examined. The pollen analysis revealed none of the pollen types that one would expect to find in the region of France where the antique chest was purportedly made or used. Although the pollen evidence did not prove the antique was a fake, it created doubt and led the owner to pursue additional tests, which eventually revealed that the item was indeed a fake. If the locks had been changed at some point after the item had been made, the original pollen evidence would have been lost.

We started this book with an example of how wood analysis helped to trap a killer, so it is fitting that we should end the book with two examples of the use of wood analysis to confirm the authenticity of an artefact. The first example concerns the authenticity and provenance of stringed instruments such as violins made by Stradivarius. Most European stringed instruments are made from spruce that has very clear growth rings. The thickness of each ring depends on the weather during each season of growth. Analysts called dendrochronologists measure the width of each ring in the varnished wood and compare the pattern with those in a database of thousands of other instruments. They also compare the pattern with that in cores extracted from very old trees and ancient timber. The year of the most recent ring on an instrument is the earliest year when it could have been made. Using this technique there have been a number of surprises such as wood from the same tree having been used by three different violin makers: one in Cremona, one in Venice and one in Madrid.

The second story begins in the 1980s when broadcaster Sir David Attenborough spotted a strange wooden figurine in an auction room in New York. According to the auction catalogue, the carving had been put up for sale by a junk shop dealer in Pennsylvania. The figurine failed to reach its reserve price but Attenborough made an offer for it after the auction and this was accepted. Having purchased it, Attenborough then began searching books on Pacific art to determine its origin and decided that it came from Easter Island. If it was genuine it would be worth a lot more than he paid but it could be just a cheap fake.

The figurine was taken to Kew Gardens where the scientists removed a small piece of wood from its base. Their analysis indicated that the wood was from the toromiro tree (*Sophora toromiro*). This tree was restricted to Easter Island but heavy deforestation resulted in it becoming extinct by 1958 when Kon-Tiki explorer Thor Heyerdahl collected seeds from the last surviving tree. This strongly suggests that the figurine is an authentic carving of an Easter Island god. Attenborough could find only one other carving that resembled his and that was in a St Petersburg museum. Records showed that before it was in St Petersburg it was in the Russian admiralty museum but how did it get there?

Johann Forster was a naturalist who sailed with Captain Cook. Attenborough was searching through the journals of Forster when he came across a precise description of his figurine and the Russian one. During a stop in Easter Island, Cook's sailors were offered carvings as barter but the only person to take any was the ship's Tahitian interpreter, Mahine. Mahine left the ship when it called at Tahiti taking the figurines with him. In 1820, the Russian explorer Fabian von Bellingshausen was commanding the sloop Vostok when it docked in Tahiti en route to the Antarctic. Tahiti's King Pomare was desperate to get linen and exchanged the Easter Island figurines for bed sheets. The figurines duly made their way back to Russia. But how did one of them end up in a Pennsylvania junk shop…?